EYEWITNESS
VIETNAM WAR

VC guerrillas ambush demonstration

Vietminh medal for bravery

Soviet-made RPG-7 grenade launcher

US lensatic military compass

US military dog tags

Peace-symbol button

Montagnard crossbow and arrows

Chinese-made penicillin, used by the Viet Cong

USS *Maddox* uniform patch

EYEWITNESS
VIETNAM WAR

Written by
STUART MURRAY

Lyndon B. Johnson
1964 campaign
button

North
Vietnamese Air
Force symbol

North
Vietnamese
stamp

AN/PRC-25 backpack
field radio

Penguin
Random
House

REVISED EDITION

DK DELHI
Senior Art Editor Vikas Chauhan
Assistant Editor Vandana Likhmania
Assistant Art Editor Prateek Maurya
Team Lead, Picture Research Sumedha Chopra
Deputy Manager, Picture Research Virien Chopra
Deputy Managing Editor Sreshtha Bhattacharya
Managing Editor Kingshuk Ghoshal
Managing Art Editor Govind Mittal
DTP Designer Vijay Kandwal
Production Editor Pawan Kumar
Senior Jackets Designer Rashika Kachroo
Creative Head Malavika Talukder

DK LONDON
Project Editor Edward Pearce **Art Editor** Chrissy Checketts
US Editor Amber Williams **US Executive Editor** Lori Cates Hand
Managing Editor Francesca Baines **Managing Art Editor** Philip Letsu
Production Controller Jack Matts
Publisher Andrew Macintyre
Art Director Mabel Chan

Consultant David L. Anderson
Sensitivity Reader Bianca Hezekiah

FIRST EDITION

DK PUBLISHING, INC.
Senior Editor Barbara Berger **Senior Designer** Tai Blanche
Additional Design Jeremy Canceko, Jee Chang, and Jessica Lasher
Assistant Managing Art Editor Michelle Baxter
Creative Director Tina Vaughan **Jacket Art Director** Dirk Kaufman
Production Manager Ivor Parker **DTP Coordinator** Milos Orlovic

MEDIA PROJECTS, INC.
Executive Editor Carter Smith **Project Editor** Aaron R. Murray
Associate Editor Margaret C. F. McLaughlin
Production Manager James A. Burmester
Consultants Clifford J. Rogers and Steve R. Waddell,
United States Military Academy
Cartography Ron Toelke, Rob Stokes
Picture Researcher Erika Rubel
Copy Editor Glenn Novak

This American Edition, 2025
First American Edition, 2005
Published in the United States by DK Publishing,
a division of Penguin Random House LLC
1745 Broadway, 20th Floor, New York, NY 10019

A catalog record for this book
is available from the Library of Congress.
ISBN 978-0-5939-6428-6 (Paperback)
ISBN 978-0-5939-6429-3 (ALB)

DK books are available at special discounts when purchased in bulk
for sales promotions, premiums, fund-raising, or educational use.
For details, contact: DK Publishing Special Markets,
1745 Broadway, 20th Floor, New York, NY 10019
SpecialSales@dk.com

Printed and bound in Malaysia

www.dk.com

M-1
bayonet

US infantry
helmet

South Vietnamese
200-dong note,
1966

Soviet-made
antitank land
mine

Chinese
cobra

US M-16A1
assault rifle

Contents

Indochina War

During World War II, Japan took control of France's colonies in Southeast Asia, then called Indochina. In 1945, Vietnamese nationalists, led by Ho Chi Minh, a Communist, battled Japanese forces for independence. Known as the Vietminh, they worked with US agents against Japan. After Japan's defeat, Ho declared Vietnam independent, but the French refused to recognize this, and tried to reclaim control.

Japanese warships

Japan's battleships patrol the waters as troops on land fight the Vietminh. Ho Chi Minh's army gained valuable experience fighting the Japanese.

Cheering crowd

Crowds pack Hanoi's Bao Dinh Square to hear Ho Chi Minh declare independence on September 2, 1945.

Japanese "Rising Sun" battle flag

Vietminh training

A US military adviser watches Vietminh fighters throwing grenades. The Vietminh included Communists and non-Communists. After the war, Ho Chi Minh won support from Communist China and the Soviet Union (USSR).

> "Our people have broken the chains which for nearly a century have fettered them and have won independence for Vietnam."
> —HO CHI MINH

Declaring independence

Ho Chi Minh speaks in Hanoi on the day of Japan's surrender. He declared an independent Democratic Republic of Vietnam (DRV), but France offered more limited freedoms. As clashes broke out and war became inevitable, the US backed France.

French military parade

French soldiers in Hanoi drive past cheering French colonial residents and Vietnamese supporters. France tried to retake control in Indochina after World War II. Some Vietnamese favored French rule. Many French-allied Vietnamese were educated in Europe and had converted to Catholicism.

Truman and Acheson

US Secretary of State Dean Acheson, right, persuaded US President Harry S. Truman, left, to give aid to France. Both men believed that Communist rule in Vietnam would lead other countries in the region to become Communist.

INDOCHINA TIMELINE

1940	Japan takes over French Indochina.
1941	Ho Chi Minh establishes the Vietminh, the "League for the Independence of Vietnam."
1945	Japan surrenders. Ho Chi Minh forms the Democratic Republic of Vietnam (DRV).
1946	French troops clash with DRV forces, sparking the First Indochina War.
1950	France suffer defeats; US sets up the Military Assistance Advisory Group (MAAG).
1951	France controls cities; Vietminh, countryside.
1954	Vietminh take Dien Bien Phu and defeat the French, ending First Indochina War. Treaty divides Vietnam into North and South.

Parachuting in

French paratroopers land at Dien Bien Phu in late 1953 to set up a new base. By spring, the Vietminh had dragged cannons up the mountains to destroy the airfield, and ground attacks were capturing French positions.

Continued from previous page

France loses Indochina

American military support helped the French gain territory early in the First Indochina War. But, after reorganizing the army and taking aid from China, a Vietminh force of 55,000 men under General Vo Nguyen Giap besieged a 15,000-strong French army in its mountain base at Dien Bien Phu. After 55 days, Colonel Christian de Castries was forced to surrender.

French defeat

Ho Chi Minh, left, and General Vo Nguyen Giap, right, study the layout of Dien Bien Phu, on the Laos border. Although the French won several clashes during the war, in the end, Giap and Ho were better strategists.

Exhausted defenders

French troops held out for 55 days under siege. About 2,000 French and 8,000 Vietminh were killed, with 10,800 French taken prisoner—most of whom died of hunger and disease.

Communist flag

The Geneva Accords

The French and Vietminh signed peace terms in Geneva, Switzerland. Called the Geneva Accords, they granted the Communists control of Vietnam north of the 17th parallel. A non-Communist government ruled South Vietnam. Elections were to be held within two years. The United States opposed a Communist-led Vietnam and refused to accept the terms or an election.

Decisive defeat

Vietnamese fighters celebrate taking Colonel de Castries's Dien Bien Phu command center on May 7, 1954. This, combined with the ambush and almost complete destruction of France's Groupement Mobile 100 battalion in late June, marked the end of the First Indochina War.

Indochina truce

Former French general Henri Delteil signs truce documents on July 20, 1954, ending hostilities. A European official and Vietnamese delegates look on in Geneva's Palace of Nations.

Vietminh medal for bravery

Victory parade

In October 1954, triumphant Vietminh troops are cheered by crowds in Hanoi. French forces had recently left for South Vietnam. After nearly eight years of war, the city became North Vietnam's capital.

North Vietnam

17th parallel

South Vietnam

Value of stamp

Communist star

Divided Vietnam

This North Vietnamese stamp shows North and South Vietnam separated by a line at the 17th parallel. The former French colonies Laos and Cambodia are to the left.

DIEN BIEN PHU TO ARMISTICE

- **1953** French troops number 90,000, with 100,000 Vietnamese National Army (colonial) troops; 200,000 Vietminh forces.
- **November 1953** France builds base at Dien Bien Phu.
- **December 1953** French troops sent to base.
- **February 1954** Giap surrounds base.
- **March 13, 1954** Ground assaults begin.
- **May 1, 1954** Final ground attacks start.
- **May 7, 1954** Dien Bien Phu falls.
- **June 24–July 17, 1954** Vietminh wipe out a French armored unit of 3,000 men.
- **August 1, 1954** Armistice.

US advisers

In 1955, President Eisenhower sent 700 military advisers to the Republic of (South) Vietnam (RVN) and helped anti-Communist Ngo Dinh Diem win power in a corrupt election. South Vietnamese Communist guerrillas—the National Liberation Front (NLF) or Viet Cong (VC)—fought Diem's government. From 1960, new US president John F. Kennedy increased American involvement in Vietnam, but in 1963, both Diem and Kennedy were assassinated.

Fleeing
Refugees from northern Vietnam rush southward in 1954, leaving behind the new Communist government, with hopes of a safe and secure life.

Jungle waters
US advisers and troops from the Army of the Republic of Vietnam (ARVN) cross a river—by 1963, 14,000 US advisers were in Vietnam.

Grenade launcher

US Army-issue helmet

First president
Diem speaks at his 1955 inauguration. A Roman Catholic, he favored other Catholics even though 80 percent of Vietnam was Buddhist.

An angry protest
Buddhist protesters in Saigon struggle with police at a demonstration against Diem in 1963. They objected to persecution of their religion and called for peaceful negotiations with the Communists.

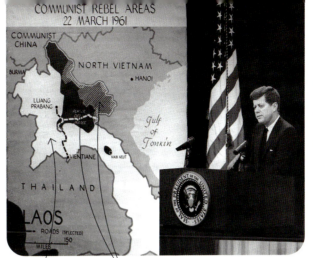

JFK'S war

US President Kennedy speaks in 1961 about the Communist threat in Southeast Asia. During his presidency, over $500 million in military aid flowed each year to South Vietnam, despite his dislike of its corrupt government.

Battle plan

Colonel John Paul Vann, left, reviews a map with ARVN and US officers. Vann was a key figure in the US Military Assistance Advisory Group (MAAG), which oversaw advisers. He objected to the careless use of firepower and preferred winning over the people.

Laos

Communist regions of Laos are shaded

MAAG uniform patch

General Duong Van Minh

Conspirators

On November 1, 1963, ARVN generals led by Duong Van Minh murdered President Diem and took power. As US involvement increased, the republic was rocked by military coups (overthrows).

Kennedy assassination

President and Mrs. Kennedy were riding in a motorcade through Dallas on November 22, 1963, when he was killed by a sniper. Vice President Lyndon B. Johnson took over the presidency.

Chicago Daily News front page coverage of JFK's assassination

Gulf of Tonkin

On August 7, 1964, Congress passed the Gulf of Tonkin Resolution, which gave President Lyndon B. Johnson (LBJ) the power to escalate US involvement in Vietnam without declaring war. This followed a North Vietnamese attack on US destroyer *Maddox* five days earlier, and US air strikes in retaliation. LBJ was now committed to waging war.

GULF OF TONKIN

* North Vietnamese cities attacked by US airstrikes
* US ship attacked by NVA patrol boats
— US air attacks

The 1964 torpedo-boat attack on the *Maddox* was an attempt to drive off US warships supporting secret assaults on North Vietnamese naval bases. Two nights later, US forces mistakenly thought another attack was underway, and LBJ ordered airstrikes.

USS *Maddox* jacket patch

USS *Maddox* officers
Captain John J. Herrick, left, headed a destroyer unit that included the *Maddox*. The commanding officer was Herbert L. Ogier, right. The unit was part of the Operation Desoto patrol.

The Tonkin clash
The *Maddox*, right, was a World War II-era destroyer modernized for electronic surveillance. It was attacked while stationed 4 miles (6 km) off an island base for North Vietnamese patrol boats. The US Navy claimed that these were international waters, so it had a right to be there.

McNamara defends war

US Secretary of Defense Robert S. McNamara explains the *Maddox* clash to reporters. Because of the Gulf of Tonkin Incident, the United States would be "moving substantial military reinforcements" to Southeast Asia.

Air campaign

Warplanes prepare to take off from the aircraft carrier USS *Constellation* in August 1964. US bombers struck naval bases in the Gulf of Tonkin. In 1965, air attacks expanded into Operation Rolling Thunder, the bombing of supply routes and munitions storage areas.

Americanizing the conflict

Although there was no declaration of war, LBJ used his war powers to their fullest, in a policy known as the Americanization of the war. In addition to the Rolling Thunder bombing campaign (see pp. 20–21), he sent troops to South Vietnam. The first Marines arrived near Da Nang in March 1965 and soon saw action against the Viet Cong. The Americanization phase of the Second Indochina War—known as the Vietnam War—had begun. By July 1965, more than 50,000 US troops were in South Vietnam.

Marines at the beach

US marines splash ashore near Da Nang, South Vietnam. More forces were arriving elsewhere, and American television showed many of these events. This was the first military conflict to be seen on television.

Under fire

This photo taken from the *Maddox* shows a speeding North Vietnamese torpedo boat as shells from the warship land nearby. Three highspeed boats launched torpedoes at the *Maddox*; its guns damaged all three. Planes from the USS *Ticonderoga* joined the fight.

North Vietnamese torpedo boat

Shell from Maddox falling into water

Allies

Allies were crucial for the Communists. The US and South Vietnam could have waged war alone, but North Vietnam and the Viet Cong needed supplies and financing from China and the Soviet Union. American and RVN forces were aided by Free World Forces (FWF): nations in the Southeast Asia Treaty Organization (SEATO). South Korea sent 312,000 troops; Australia sent 47,000. Thailand, the Philippines, and New Zealand also sent soldiers.

Allied propaganda
In this South Vietnamese poster, flags represent the Allied nations. They offer food to the Vietnamese, while the Soviet Union offers only guns.

Medal
The text reads: "Solidarity against American aggression."

A warm welcome in China
North Vietnamese officials receive an enthusiastic greeting from Premier Zhou Enlai on a state visit to Beijing in 1973.

Chinese munitions
This Chinese-made 4.72-in (120-mm) mortar round was captured at a VC supply base in Cambodia.

Ho in Russia
Ho Chi Minh joins Soviet officials and leaders from other Communist states at a military parade in Moscow in 1961.

Cuban Communist Party leader Blas Roca

President Ho Chi Minh

Soviet premier Nikita Khrushchev

Hungarian party leader János Kádár

Soviet president Leonid Brezhnev

RVN prime minister Nguyen Cao Ky

Australian prime minister Harold Holt

Philippine president Ferdinand Marcos

South Korean president Park Chung Hee

New Zealand prime minister Keith Holyoake

Thai prime minister Thanom Kittikachorn

RVN chief of state Nguyen Van Thieu

US president Lyndon B. Johnson

SEATO leaders in the Philippines

Heads of SEATO nations and nonmembers South Korea and South Vietnam meet in Manila to discuss the Indochina conflict in October 1966. SEATO was founded in 1954 under US direction to prevent the spread of Communism in the region.

More than 60,000
Australian troops fought in the Vietnam War from 1962 to 1973.

Awards

President Marcos pins medals on Filipino soldiers in July 1967, at the US base in Tay Ninh, South Vietnam. Filipino troops arrived in Indochina in 1966.

Australian service medal

Ambush

The 7th Australian Royal Regiment sets up an ambush in hill country. The "Aussies" usually operated guerrilla-style. In 1966, a 101-man combat team fought off more than 2,500 VC at Long Tan.

Flower wreath given to welcome the president

Free World Forces hang tag

This I.D. tag was attached to a button and worn on the shirts of troops that the Allies called Free World Forces (FWF).

South Korean troops

Koreans guard VC prisoners, c.1966. South Korea had the third-largest Allied army in Vietnam, after the US and South Vietnam.

The leaders

At the start of the war, Vietnamese Communist leaders had been in power for more than 20 years and had vast military experience. US and South Vietnamese leaders were mostly politicians. Ho Chi Minh and Vo Nguyen Giap stayed in power for much of the war, while US and RVN leaders came and went. While Communists fought all-out, the US conducted a "limited war," trying to use enough force to make the enemy surrender.

"Uncle Ho"

Ho's struggle against French and Japanese occupation prepared him for the Vietnam War. He died before the final Communist triumph in 1975.

Vo Nguyen Giap

General Giap led Communist forces from the 1940s to 1972. Younger generals took over late in the war. Giap retired as minister of defense in 1980.

Le Duan

Le Duan, a tough southern Vietminh leader, became first secretary of the Workers Party in 1960. He ran the DRV military effort during the war.

"We are determined to fight for independence, national unity, democracy, and peace."

—*HO CHI MINH*

Tran Do

Deputy commander of Viet Cong forces in South Vietnam, Tran Do was a high-ranking member of the Communist Party. He later fell out with the Communist-led government.

Pham Van Dong

One of the founders of the Indochinese Communist Party, Dong, right, became North Vietnam's prime minister in 1955.

Nguyen Van Thieu

Shown voting in an election, Thieu was president of South Vietnam from 1967 to 1973. In the First Indochina War, he fought first for the Vietminh, but then joined the French colonial forces. He later rose to power in South Vietnam. Thieu often tried to control ARVN units in the field, angering his generals.

Nguyen Cao Ky

A South Vietnamese pilot and air force leader, General Ky was the premier in President Thieu's government from 1965 to 1971. When Saigon fell in 1975, he fled to America.

William C. Westmoreland

General Westmoreland was commander of US forces in Vietnam when the first US combat troops landed in 1965. He was replaced in 1968.

Nixon and Kissinger

President Richard Nixon, left, discusses peace talks with special adviser Henry Kissinger in 1972. Elected in 1968, Nixon chose to prolong the war rather than withdraw and admit defeat.

"We have no ambition there for ourselves, we seek no wider war."

—*LYNDON B. JOHNSON*

Lyndon B. Johnson

Lyndon B. Johnson

Johnson feared being the president who let Vietnam become Communist. He is seen here with advisers on *Air Force One*, after meeting South Vietnamese leaders in Hawaii.

Lyndon B. Johnson campaign button

Saigon **and Hanoi**

The capital of French Indochina, Hanoi had long been a political, cultural, and economic center. In 1954, it became the DRV's capital. Saigon, South Vietnam's capital, soon surpassed it in wealth and population, becoming the military headquarters and benefiting from US aid. Hanoi teemed with bicycles, Saigon with cars and scooters; military vehicles soon appeared in both.

Hanoi politicians
Prime Minister Pham Van Dong, center, attends a government meeting in Hanoi in 1946. Communists dominated the government.

Hanoi

Colonial Hanoi was famous for its restaurants and stylish upper class. After independence, it became a manufacturing hub with top schools and hospitals. Its citizens had suffered to overthrow the French, but fought on in the war to unify the nation.

Women home guards
An official registers women in Hanoi's home guard in 1964. The guard's role was to protect the city during conflicts. This often included operating antiaircraft weaponry.

TWO VIETNAMS

NORTH VIETNAM · CHINA · Hanoi · Haiphong · Red River · Gulf of Tonkin · CHINA · LAOS · Vinh · Demilitarized Zone (DMZ) · Hué · Da Nang · THAILAND · Kontum · SOUTH VIETNAM · CAMBODIA · Ban Me Thuot · Central Highlands · Phnom Penh · Tay Ninh · Saigon · Mekong River · Mekong Delta · South China Sea

■ North Vietnam
■ South Vietnam

A major seaport, Saigon was strongly influenced by foreign cultures. Hanoi was influenced by neighboring giant China.

Hanoi in peaceful times
In the period before independence in 1954, few North Vietnamese owned motorized vehicles. Bicycles and pushcarts crowded the streets. Hanoi would soon start to become a center for government, industry, and higher education.

Saigon

Under the French, Saigon became a modern city with a Vietnamese Roman Catholic elite—most Vietnamese were Buddhist. In 1955, it became the RVN capital and grew rapidly, as 900,000 people fled Communist North Vietnam—by 1965, its population was 1.5 million. Saigon was notorious for corruption, gambling, and opium.

Saigon's old town

The influence of 19th-century French colonial culture is seen in this 1955 street scene. The city's culture, architecture, and nightlife earned it the nickname "Paris of the East."

Heroes returning

Battle-weary ARVN soldiers marching in a Saigon parade in 1961 are given garlands of flowers. The troops had been operating against VC insurgents.

Scrip and stolen goods

"Scrip," or special bills given to US forces to buy goods on military bases, were traded like dollars, and stolen US goods were also openly sold.

American goods, smuggled or stolen for the black market

Bustling boulevard

Saigon streets were clogged with scooters and cars in the mid-1960s. Still, the three-wheeled "peditaxi" was a prime means of transportation. Carts powered by cyclists were also essential in the overcrowded city.

Rolling Thunder

After the Gulf of Tonkin incident, the US launched Operation Rolling Thunder in March 1965 to bomb power plants, fuel depots, railroads, airfields, and factories. LBJ halted the attacks seven times, on each occasion hoping the Communists would ask for peace. They did not, and on October 31, 1968, Johnson ended the operation.

Air Force Thunderchiefs

Air Force F-105 Thunderchief fighter-bombers refuel in the air while on their way to bomb North Vietnam in 1966. The refueling aircraft, top right, is a KC-135 Stratotanker.

389th Tactical Fighter Squadron patch

TARGETS

CHINA

NORTH VIETNAM

Hanoi

Haiphong

Gulf of Tonkin

From Thailand

From S. Vietnam

B-52s from Okinawa

B-52s from Guam

Demilitarized Zone (DMZ)

THAILAND

SOUTH VIETNAM

US 7th Fleet

- ▨ Chinese buffer zone (prohibited to US aircraft)
- ◯ Target restrictions around Hanoi and Haiphong
- ▬ US air attacks

Operation Rolling Thunder saw at least 643,000 tons (583,300 metric tons) of bombs dropped. Planes avoided heavily populated areas to limit civilian casualties.

A-1 Skyraider warplane

Folding wings for storage on aircraft carrier deck

Successful mission

Navy commander George Jacobssen Jr. signals "okay" after a mission against NVA ammunition depots in 1965. During Rolling Thunder, US planes were restricted to military and economic targets.

Bombs fall

F-105 Thunderchiefs following a B-66 Destroyer over North Vietnam drop their bombs. The fighter-bombers flew low to avoid NVA radar and hit targets with accuracy; high-flying heavy bombers dropped payloads over a wider area.

After a strike

A rail bridge is damaged after a US air strike. Cutting railroads made it hard for the Communists to move equipment and troops. Whenever LBJ halted bombing, the North Vietnamese rebuilt.

Bridge collapsed from precision bombing

Wild Weasel landing

F-100 "Wild Weasel" fighters' radar-jamming equipment interfered with antiaircraft electronic devices. Flying daringly low, they specialized in attacking surface-to-air missile (SAM) sites.

Wild Weasel patch

Parachute slows plane

Air defense

With Soviet and Chinese aid, especially planes and antiaircraft weapons, Hanoi built a formidable defense that saw its air force in particular become increasingly effective. The US, meanwhile, dropped more bombs during Rolling Thunder than it had in the Pacific Theater in World War II.

B-66 Destroyer, a light bomber.

Home guard

Women in the Hanoi home guard search the skies for US warplanes. Civilians were given weapons and instructed to fire into the air, creating a storm of bullets.

Explosive warhead

Aiming a SAM

A surface-to-air missile crew prepares for action. Thousands of Chinese SAM operators volunteered to serve in North Vietnam. SAMs contained 250 lb (114 kg) of explosives. The US lost 922 aircraft, many shot down by SAMs.

Air-raid alarm

A Hanoi resident takes cover in an air-raid shelter. Sirens alerted people to find shelter immediately when US planes were nearby.

Ho Chi Minh Trail

This wilderness route took Communist supplies and troops to South Vietnam. The main trail ran from Hanoi into Laos, while another branch started in Cambodia. Much of the 12,500-mile (20,000-km) trail was paved. There were underground barracks, hospitals, munitions storage, and, later in the war, 3,000 miles (5,000 km) of fuel pipeline. By 1970, 20,000 tons (18,000 metric tons) of supplies were moved every month.

VAST ROUTE

Both Laos and Cambodia stayed neutral during the war. Cambodia's Prince Norodom Sihanouk did not want to anger the Communists by blocking the trail, part of which was nicknamed "Sihanouk Trail."

The trail was so dangerous that it was sometimes called **"the blood road."**

Laying steel

North Vietnamese Army (NVA) engineers fight rushing waters to lay steel girders for a bridge in 1966. Roads and bridges for trucks replaced paths and river fords. Designed by the NVA's Logistics Group 559, the project took more than 100,000 workers to build and maintain.

Wooden staircase tied together with rope

Stairway to war

NVA troops walk down cliffside steps near the DMZ in 1966. It will take two months for the unit to march to its final position in South Vietnam. The Ho Chi Minh Trail was also called the "Truong Son Road" because it entered the Truong Son Mountains of central Vietnam.

Bicycle warfare

Laborers on the Ho Chi Minh Trail used bicycles to haul ammunition. The bikes had special handles for easier steering. The Communists could not have waged war without the trail to move supplies.

Sulfa drugs

The NVA used sulfa drugs sent by the USSR to treat engineers, soldiers, and laborers for bacterial and parasitic infections and malaria.

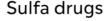

Mountain pass

Communist troops cross misty mountains near the Laos border. As many as 20,000 NVA troops trekked south on the Ho Chi Minh Trail every month. Thousands died from air raids, disease, snake bites, and even tigers.

Viet Cong sandals

US and ARVN soldiers had modern gear. Communist guerrillas used what they could salvage. These sandals were cut from old rubber tires.

Road for trucks

Supply trucks pass through a defoliated part of the trail in the 1970s. Trucks became the heart of the transport system. Engineering battalions had worked by hand at first, but later got Soviet and Chinese roadbuilding equipment.

Chemicals in **war**

The US wanted to eliminate Viet Cong support in the countryside by destroying food supplies and driving out locals who aided the VC. The policy of defoliation—killing vegetation with chemical poisons—was enacted to expose tree-covered guerrilla bases and supply routes. Agent Orange was sprayed over vast areas. Napalm and white phosphorus (WP) bombs also turned lush landscapes into wastelands.

Making napalm

A US soldier makes napalm, using chemical thickeners. On exploding, flaming globules of jellylike napalm stick to all they touch, including skin, causing great suffering.

Destructive payload

Napalm bombs are mounted under the wing of a bomber at Da Nang airfield. Napalm was first used in World War II.

Flames of war

Liquid fire blossoms into fireballs as a napalm and WP strike blasts a VC hamlet in 1965. The clinging flames of a napalm attack burn for hours on trees and buildings. Napalm was widely used by the US in Vietnam.

Napalm explosion

Ranch Hand's assault

Lasting from 1962 to 1971, the defoliation campaign Operation Ranch Hand began with six aircraft but had 25 by its peak in 1969. Low-flying craft targeted VC bases in Cambodia and South Vietnam, spraying jungles and crops. In all, it used 19 million gallons (72 million liters) of herbicides—60 percent was Agent Orange.

Trail of defoliant spray

Patch

Members of the 12th Air Command Squadron wore this patch from late 1966.

Before and after

The effects of defoliation are seen in this aerial photograph. The field on the right side of the river is brown after being poisoned with Agent Orange. The left bank is still a vibrant green.

Poisonous spray

Agent Orange can cause illness in humans. US service members and Vietnamese civilians had lasting health problems from contact with the herbicide.

Machine gunner

Chopper spray

A Huey helicopter sprays defoliant in the Mekong Delta in 1969. The U Minh Forest of mangrove swamps had a dense canopy that hid people and buildings from aircraft. Herbicides killed this, exposing the VC position.

Most jungles could recover from two sprayings, but not three. **Mangrove swamps** died after a single spraying.

Sampan propelled by oars

River through ruin

A man paddles his boat between the bare banks of a former mangrove forest in the Mekong Delta in 1970. Agent Orange destroyed swamps that were once bountiful for fishing.

Highlands
struggle

In Vietnam's Central Highlands—between Cambodia and the sea—US and Allied forces attacked VC and NVA strongholds. American bases were under constant threat, and troops operating in the dense forests were often ambushed. Communists planned to cut off and capture South Vietnam's northern provinces, but lost major battles in the Ia Drang Valley and at Dak To.

THE CENTRAL HIGHLANDS

Highland valleys could lead Communist forces to the coast. US bases fought to block enemy movements.

Dak To
Kontum
Duc Co
Pleiku
LZ X-Ray and LZ Albany
Phu Cat
Ia Drang Valley
CAMBODIA
Central Highlands
Ban Me Thuot
SOUTH VIETNAM

✴ Battle sites
— Main roads

N W E S

NVA forces

NVA troops occupied large areas of the Central Highlands. They were trained in wilderness fighting and could move swiftly and silently. The Americans and ARVN, however, won the major engagements during most of the war.

NVA helmet
NVA soldiers wore light but sturdy helmets that protected them from sun and rain.

Tube scarf
NVA soldiers carried their daily ration of rice in a tubelike scarf that kept it secure.

Nguyen Chi Thanh
General Thanh led a major NVA offensive in the Highlands in 1965. He aimed for the sea, but his forces were stopped at Ia Drang Valley.

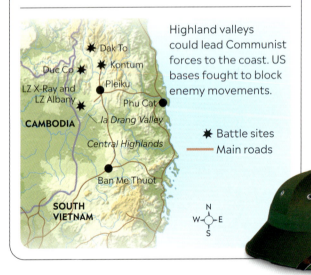

Ammo pouch
This ammunition belt is typical NVA "webbing," the term for military belts and pouches made of fabric.

Fastening loop

NVA canteen
Communists carried little gear compared to Allied troops. They had to move fast and live off the land; a water canteen was vital.

Free World Fo[rces]

Like the Communists, Free W[orld]
Forces (FWF) used assault rifles [and]
grenade launchers. FWF weaponry w[as]
matched by the NVA's, but was supe[rior]
to the VC's. FWF also had the advan[tage]
of artillery and resupply from the ai[r, while]
the VC relied on the Ho Chi Minh Tra[il.]

M-16 cleaning kit

Firearms must be cleaned and oiled to work. This US M-16 kit is used to swab the barrel.

Barr[el]
gre[nade]
laun[cher]

Handle for cleaning ro[d]

Cle[aning]

Cleaning brush attaches to rod

Hinge to fold rod compactly into a pouch

Cleaning brush

US grenades

The infantry carried grenades. The ring for the pin was pulled, and after it was thrown, a fuse would light. Seconds later, it exploded.

Pineapple grenade

Baseball grenade

Lemon grenade

155-mm howitzer

ARVN artillerymen used the 155-mm howitzer. Shells take a high trajectory, so defenses that resist direct fire are vulnerable to shells dropping from above.

Setting up a highland base

A Chinook transport helicopter supplies US Airmobile troopers at a new mountaintop base in 1967. The Americans are on a search-and-destroy operation. The landing zone is code-named LZ Quick, which the NVA tried to ambush.

Montagnard men

Montagnard soldiers armed with US submachine guns prepare for patrol. Special Forces teams began training Montagnards as early as 1963, during the advisory period of the Vietnam War.

Elite forces and allies

Small teams of US "Green Beret" Special Forces used guerrilla tactics and allied with the local Montagnards ("mountain peoples" in French), whom they equipped and trained. Now known as the Dega, these fiercely independent peoples initially opposed both NVA and RVN. Other US elite forces in the area included Air Cavalry and Airborne troopers.

Chopper landing

A Green Beret waves in a supply helicopter. The US Special Forces' isolated mountain bases were supplied by air, but the men often lived off the land. They faced danger daily.

Land navigation

This soldier wears a position locator to find his way. The device's pedometer step sensor helps him work out where he is by measuring stride length.

AIRBORNE

Green Beret Airborne patch

Taking aim

This 101st Airborne trooper is under fire in the battle of Dak To. Fierce fighting lasted three weeks. Victory came on Thanksgiving Day, 1967.

Crossbow bolts

Quiver

Wooden body

Crossbow

This traditional Montagnard weapon could be deadly in counterguerrilla warfare. It fired short arrows called bolts.

Weapc

The war was waged with b
US firearms were matche
VC also used booby traps
to VC resistance in the So
spent shell casings and se
by ground action that rec

Bomb-making
VC soldiers salvage US shell casings and unexploded artillery ammo. They reload the casings to make explosive devices. Grenades were put in booby traps.

Gr

Grenade launcher
The rocket-propelled grenade launcher (RPG) fires warheads that can penetrate armor, destroying armored trucks and tanks.

R

Warhead holds explosive

Trigger and magazine

SKS Sir
The bayon
into a supp
fired lying

On **patrol**

The fighting in Vietnam required foot soldiers. Soldiers patrolled villages to protect locals from the VC or NVA, who often lay in wait. Reconnaissance missions—by platoons or companies of 20 to 100 men—were done to learn about enemy units. The aim of search-and-destroy missions was to kill or capture the enemy. In a firefight, the commander radioed for air or artillery support.

Bearings
An infantryman on patrol in unfamiliar territory uses a compass to determine his location. The Lensatic military compass has a front sight and a magnifying lens and folds into a carrying case.

Sighting wire, used with rear-sight slot and lens to sight on objects

Rear-sight slot

Lens is used to magnify dial

Waterproof material

Jungle boots
Waterproof boots were needed for patrolling in swampy jungles.

Bug repellent

Infantry helmet
The helmet strap could hold Army-issue cigarettes and bug repellent.

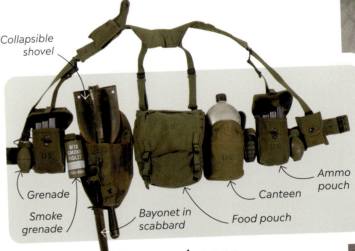

Collapsible shovel

Grenade

Smoke grenade

Bayonet in scabbard

Food pouch

Canteen

Ammo pouch

Day-pack gear
Fully loaded, this gear belt for day patrol is 60 lb (27 kg). It holds ammo, a shovel, bayonet, canteen, first-aid kit, and food.

In the open
Troops of the 9th Infantry Division turn toward possible enemy movement as they walk across a rice paddy. Patrols were exposed to attack, especially as they entered forests, villages, or open fields. This is a day patrol, since the soldiers carry little gear. Long-range reconnaissance patrols usually went into the field for days.

The soldier leading
a patrol was most in danger during an ambush.

Backpack field radio

Radio controls

Handset (phone)

Calling the base

A radioman carries a field radio as his commanding officer talks to the base. Patrols set out from fire bases—encampments with headquarters, artillery, and troops. A patrol could radio for enemy positions to be shelled or call for help.

Instructions for inflating canteen

Collecting water

A 1st Infantry Division soldier refills his canteen. Halazone, a bacteria-killing powder, was added to make the water safe to drink.

Vial of halazone

VC ambush

The Viet Cong were skilled at ambush. They hid in trees, fields, and even underground, and often struck in a hail of gunfire and grenades. The lead patrol—the man "on point"—was in particular danger. If outnumbered, the VC sought cover. Otherwise, they would try to wipe out the patrol before air support arrived.

Demonstrating tactics

Posing for the camera, VC guerrillas show how to hide in haystacks. In combat, they would disappear under the hay if an enemy patrol approached. If the patrol was too strong, they let it pass. If not, they attacked.

Medevac
"Dustoff" on this pilot's belt buckle is a nickname for ambulance helicopters.

Medical care

In 1965, the US had two 100-bed military hospitals in Vietnam. By 1969, 30 hospitals with a total of 5,000 beds and two hospital ships were staffed by 16,000 doctors, 15,000 nurses, and thousands of support staff. In battle, medics bandaged the wounded. Emergency flights could get them to hospital. In contrast, Communist wounded were carried to field hospitals hidden in swamps, caves, or tunnels.

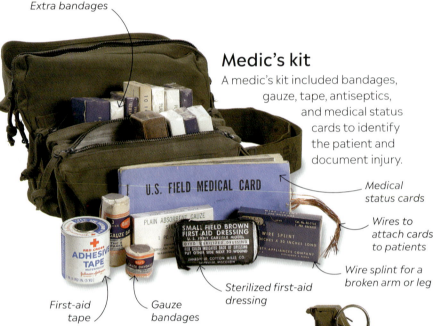

Extra bandages

Medic's kit
A medic's kit included bandages, gauze, tape, antiseptics, and medical status cards to identify the patient and document injury.

U.S. FIELD MEDICAL CARD

Medical status cards

Wires to attach cards to patients

Wire splint for a broken arm or leg

Sterilized first-aid dressing

First-aid tape

Gauze bandages

Evacuating a wounded soldier
An injured soldier is carried through the jungle. Fewer than one in five US wounded died from injuries, against one in three in World War II.

M18 SMOKE VIOLET

1701-9054

Purple smoke grenade

Medevac chopper arrives
A medevac (medical evacuation) helicopter picks up wounded troops in 1966. The pilot homes in on the purple smoke-cloud that signals where to land. Many soldiers were treated within 20 minutes of being injured.

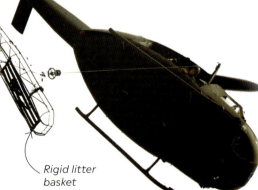

Rigid litter basket

Basket
A helicopter lowers a rigid litter basket to be loaded with an injured soldier. Often, choppers could not land in dense jungle, so litters were lowered by cable, and the wounded hauled up.

First stop

The chopper's red cross symbolizes a medical unit, which was not to be fired upon. Medevac helicopters were shot down by enemies regardless, and some were lost.

Injured in combat

More than 350,000 Purple Heart medals were awarded during the Vietnam War.

President George Washington

Dog tags

All troops wear metal "dog tags" around their necks. The tags are stamped with the soldier's personal data.

Saving a life

A surgical team operates at a US field hospital in 1969. Male doctors were usually drafted; women were volunteers. Seriously injured patients were flown to US hospitals in Japan for further care.

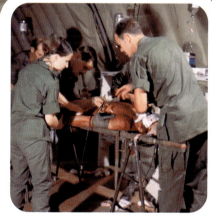

Communist med units

Communist field hospitals in South Vietnam were camouflaged to prevent bombing attacks. Sparse medical supplies came mostly from China or the USSR. Many fighters suffered greatly from tropical diseases and fever.

Chinese penicillin bottle

Journey for aid

Communist soldiers carry a wounded comrade on a hammock litter suspended on a bamboo pole through difficult terrain to a field hospital.

Hammock attached to a pole for carrying patients

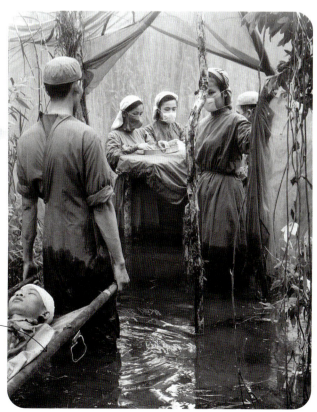

Wood-and-canvas stretcher

Operating in a swamp

VC nurses and doctors work knee-deep in water in a field hospital. The stretcher-bearer brings a patient to the operating table.

Heliborne warfare

Helicopters came into wide use in Vietnam. Until then, they had been used for scouting and airlifting wounded. In the 1960s, US "choppers" were improved in power and armaments. They rushed soldiers into action, fired on the enemy, and moved supplies. The NVA had no helicopters.

M-16 rifle

Landing skids

Supply pouch

Harry Kinnard

General Kinnard led the 1st Cavalry Division— the first unit transported by helicopter. Called airmobile or heliborne troops, they went to Vietnam in 1965.

Rocket on target

US helicopters such as this Bell UH-1 "Huey" supported ground troops with covering fire from rockets and machine guns, communicating with the troops by radio.

Gunners

A machine gunner looks for VC from the air. Gunners were favorite enemy targets. Their duty was one of the most dangerous.

Cobra attack helicopter

The AH-1W Sea Cobra was one of the first attack helicopters, introduced in 1967. These "gunships" escorted fast transport helicopters. Used by the Marines and Army, Cobras were swift and agile, with great firepower.

Pilot and copilot positions

Fuselage and tail

Huey weaponry

The Huey's armaments included seven-pod aerial-rocket launchers and rapid-firing machine guns, such as the "minigun."

Pilot and copilot positions

Cannon

Insignia

Pilots and mechanics wore special patches. These units of the 7th Squadron, 1st Cavalry Regiment, called themselves "Apache Aeroscouts" and "King Birds."

Apache Aeroscouts

King Birds

Cargo helicopters

The Americans and ARVN operated thousands of helicopters during the war, with four main models: utility for general use; observation for scouting; attack gunships for battle; and cargo for transporting supplies around the country. Models were always being updated.

Air cavalry

"Air Cav" troops of the 1st Air Cavalry Division, the world's first heliborne soldiers, jump from a Iuey on a scouting mission. Their success led to the widespread use of helicopters and airmobile units.

Chinook

The mighty CH-47 Chinook was one of the best cargo aircraft of the war. These heavy-lifting helicopters often transported field guns. Here, a gun is suspended under the body of a Chinook.

Landing wheel

Cannon barrel

Field cannon

Cannon limber

Tail-mounted rotor

Rotors

Flying crane

This CH-54A Skycrane transport helicopter was dubbed a "Flying Crane" for its ability to lift heavy loads. Skycranes often moved guns and vehicles into isolated bases, where soldiers built artillery positions to prepare for battle.

Cutaway design for large cargo

Tall landing gear for cutaway

Warplanes

Rolling Thunder struck North Vietnamese roads, railroads, and bridges to slow the supply chain, but avoided cities to limit civilian casualties. Antiaircraft fire targeted US F-105 fighter-bombers. In January 1967, superior US fighters won a dramatic victory over the North's Soviet-made MiG-21s. By the end of 1967, the bombing campaign had devastated North Vietnam, but the US had lost 649 aircraft.

F-4D Phantom cockpit

Top US ace
Captain Charles DeBellevue flew 220 combat missions and shot down six MiGs.

Tricking NVAF defenders

North Vietnamese Air Force (NVAF) MiG-21s took on slower F-105s but avoided swift F-4 Phantoms. In Operation Bolo on January 2, 1967, Colonel Robin Olds led 8th Tactical Fighter Wing F-4s in formation with F-105s, using F-105 radio call signs to disguise their presence. This drew several enemy MiG-21s into action, and seven of them were shot down. No US planes were lost.

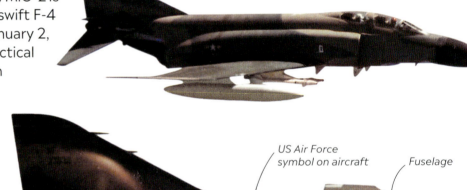

US Air Force symbol on aircraft

Fuselage

Rear horizontal wing stabilizes plane

Air-to-air missile

Colonel's eagle

Harness for parachute

Bolo leader
Colonel Robin Olds downed one of the MiG-21s in Operation Bolo. He would shoot down four aircraft in the war, earning the Air Force Cross for extraordinary heroism.

Vest with pouches

Inflation hose controls air pressure in flight suit

Flight suit

MiG killers
F-4 Phantoms fly in formation in 1967. This formidable fighter escorted older and less maneuverable F-105 fighter-bombers in missions over the North. The F-4 was the best fighter of the day, flying at 1,600 mph (2,500 kph). They were termed "MiG killers."

Air Force Cross

Bald eagle symbolizes the United States and air-striking power.

NVAF ace

Pham Thanh Ngan, a leading NVAF ace, wears a medal for each of his kills (8th medal not shown). NVAF pilots were trained by China and the USSR, who made their planes.

Air Medal

Ho Chi Minh

Medal

Pilots got this for each Allied plane shot down.

Dogfight

Viewed through the 20-mm cannon sight of a pursuing F-105, an NVAF MiG-17, above, is hit on the wing. The F-105 fighter-bombers were faster than a MiG-17, but no match for MiG-21s in aerial combat, known as dogfights. This F-105 next passed just 20 ft (6 m) beneath the doomed MiG.

Preparing for takeoff

Mai Van Cuong, another NVAF ace with eight kills, gets ready to fly. Nguyen Van Coc, the top ace, had nine kills. Pilots became aces after five kills. The NVAF's 16 aces shot down 106 of 169 US planes lost in air-to-air combat.

MiG-21 cockpit

Second cockpit for weapons system officer

Pilot's cockpit

Engine exhaust

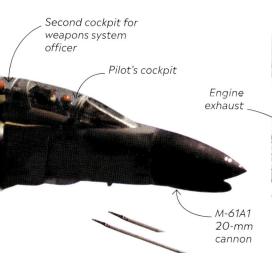

Cockpit cover

Air base

A crew services a fighter based at an NVAF airfield near Hanoi. US bombers had orders to avoid cities, so the NVAF based aircraft nearby.

M-61A1 20-mm cannon

Nose

Serial number

NVAF symbol on aircraft

Soviet MiG-21

The highly agile MiG-21 was designed to intercept attacking enemy aircraft. It flew at 1,385 mph (2,200 kph) and was armed with air-to-air missiles. Between 1965 and 1973, US warplanes downed 68 MiG-21s.

Landing gear

The Television War

The Vietnam War was called the first "Television War," as TV brought the horrors of war into homes as never before. At first, the media supported the war, reporting on the military situation, but not explaining Vietnam's struggle against foreign rule. As the conflict worsened, the government claimed it was going well. Some journalists began to call for peace.

At the typewriter
Journalist Neil Sheehan covered the war and later exposed US government lies about it.

Fighting reporter
United Press International's Joseph Galloway often fought alongside the troops he covered. He won a Bronze Star for rescuing a wounded man.

Bronze Star

Aiming with a camera
Vietnamese photographer Huynh Thanh My lies in muddy water under enemy fire while on assignment for the Associated Press (AP). My covered ARVN troops fighting in the Mekong Delta in 1965. He was killed later that year.

Interviewing soldiers
Reporters from CBS News interview US soldiers about a recent battle in 1967. Military commanders gave journalists considerable freedom to meet the troops.

Lo Manh Hung
The youngest Vietnamese photojournalist, Lo Manh Hung was only 12 when he covered war stories in Saigon during the Tet Offensive in 1968. His age allowed him to sneak through crowds to capture the best picture. Hung was taught by his father, a freelance photographer.

Helping the injured
In 1975, UPI photographer Willie Vicoy carries a wounded girl to safety after rockets hit near Cambodia's capital, Phnom Penh. Press members often helped the injured before reporting.

Stars and Stripes patch

Department of Defense seal

Press pass

War correspondents had press cards. Frances FitzGerald's reporting won her fame.

News about his war

A 9th Division soldier reads the Army's daily newspaper, *Stars and Stripes*, which tells of military action and antiwar protests. The publication was widely respected for its accurate reporting.

NVA news

VC general Tran Van Tra speaks at a press conference. Like the Allies, Communist officials limited the war information they released to the public.

Helmet with AP logo

Pentagon conference

US Secretary of Defense Robert McNamara faces journalists at the Pentagon in 1967. The government's daily press conferences often gave too-optimistic or misleading reports.

Walter Cronkite and Vietnam

In 1968, CBS anchor Cronkite dismayed many Americans by comparing the destruction and loss in Vietnam to World War II, which he had covered, and criticizing US policy. LBJ said, "If I've lost Cronkite, I've lost middle America."

Exposing the truth

In 1971, ex-Pentagon staffer Daniel Ellsberg gave *The New York Times* secret documents detailing government lies about the war. Neil Sheehan reported on these in "The Pentagon Papers." Most Americans by now wanted the war to end.

The Mekong Delta

The Mekong Delta, covered in waterlogged rice paddies, is Indochina's "rice bowl." At its mouth, the Mekong River is 26,000 square miles (67,340 sq km). It was a guerrilla stronghold in the Indochina wars. US and ARVN forces established bases there; gunboats sailed the waterways, infantry patrolled on foot, and aircraft struck VC positions. The VC held on, aided by local villagers.

MEKONG DELTA

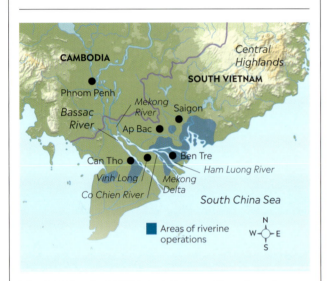

The 2,800-mile (4,500-km) Mekong River deposits fine soil as it empties into the South China Sea, building up a delta (sandy lowland). Near the Mekong Delta is Saigon, South Vietnam's largest city. The areas shaded in blue on the map show US and ARVN riverine operations against the VC.

Viet Cong fighter

Guerrilla sentry Soc Trang stands at her post in the Mekong Delta, in 1973. Trang was just 24, but had already been widowed twice. Both husbands were VC soldiers who died in action. The VC and North Vietnamese forces counted many women among their fighters in the field. Trang carries a captured US M-16 rifle.

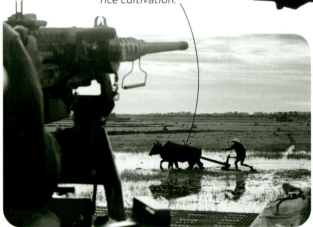

Water buffalo serve as draft animals for rice cultivation.

Under the gun

An ARVN personnel carrier's machine gun aims toward a farmer plowing his rice paddy. The government often destroyed crops to keep them from the VC, which angered farmers.

Flames from rocket strike

Strike mission

Flames and smoke rise from a rocket attack by an American UH-1A Iroquois helicopter in the Mekong Delta. Twisting waterways and patchwork rice paddies are surrounded by dense woods that shelter VC guerrillas.

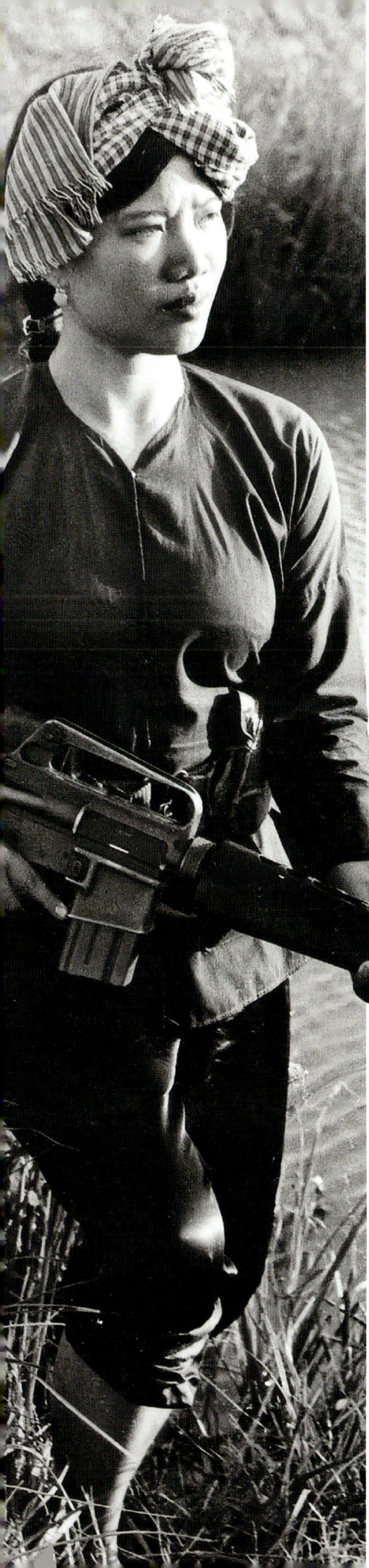

Mekong hamlet

This aerial photo shows a remote hamlet in the Mekong River in 1968. The river is just a few feet deep here. Centuries-old raised paths link the houses, but most travel is by boat.

Raised path between houses

Thatched roof

Poling homeward

A family uses poles to push a boat through the waters around their hamlet, as a neighbor builds a house. A typical home is framed with poles, has a thatched roof of dried leaves or straw, and sits on an earthen base above the water.

Poles support racks for drying fishing nets.

Captured US M-16 rifle

US soldier's patch

The 9th Infantry Division served in the Mekong. It was a difficult service, with frequent VC ambushes and a brutal climate.

Monitor in the Mekong

An armed and armored Monitor gunboat churns past a village in the Mekong Delta in an operation against the VC. The Navy gunboat is headed to a nearby base, where other military craft are gathered.

War on
inland waters

In 1965, the US Navy began patrolling South Vietnam's 3,000 miles (4,800 km) of inland waterways. The swampy Mekong and Saigon river deltas were Communist strongholds. In 1967, MACV set up the Mobile Riverine Force. This "Brown Water Navy" combined Army troops, Navy patrol boat crews, gunboats, and napalm-firing boats. Large vessels served as floating barracks.

Elmo R. Zumwalt
Called the "Father of the Brown Water Navy," Admiral Zumwalt led US naval forces in Vietnam from 1968 to 1970.

Naval patches
Each Navy unit had its own patch design, such as an eagle atop a cannon, a "River Rat," or the lightning and swords patch worn by the River Patrol Force.

River Assault Division 91 patch

USS *White River* naval patch

Patch of the River Patrol Force, Task Force 116

Gunboat
A Monitor patrols the Mekong Delta in 1967. These armored vessels were named after Union gunboats of the Civil War.

50-mm cannon

Rotating armored gun turret

Reinforced steel hull

Patrolling the Mekong
A Navy task force travels through the VC-held Mekong Delta in 1967. Armored assault boats were part of the Riverine Force. They took part in Operation Coronado and inflicted heavy losses on the enemy.

Loading ramp falls forward onto riverbank when landing troops

Thick steel armor protects troops

Pole used to propel and steer craft

ARVN ride a sampan
South Vietnamese troops, in the southern province of Ca Mau, transport firewood to a camp in a native craft. South Vietnam had a modern navy, but its riverine forces often used the traditional sampan.

A Navy Zippo blast

In ambushes, the VC often prioritized boats nicknamed "Zippos," after a popular cigarette lighter. Guns on their turrets shot streams of flaming napalm up to 200 yards (180 m), destroying everything in range.

Burning out the VC

Simple but effective, the flaming arrow being fired from this US officer's bow will set the straw roofs of a Viet Cong riverbank base on fire. Such strikes avoided the need to land troops.

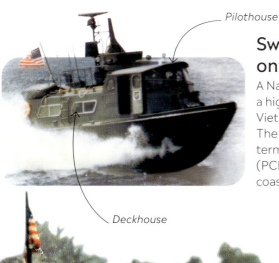

Pilothouse

Deckhouse

Swift boat on patrol

A Navy Swift boat makes a highspeed run in South Vietnam's Cam Ranh Bay. The Swifts, officially termed "patrol craft fast" (PCF), served along the coast and on inland rivers.

Shark mouth

Fiercely decorated, fast-moving patrol air-cushion vehicles (PACVs) could cross swamps and rice paddies. Hovercraft could transport troops for surprise missions and quickly block escape routes.

Shark-tooth bow design

Village life

Vietnamese villagers lived much as their ancestors had done for centuries. VC fighters relied on them and threatened those who did not cooperate. US and ARVN troops ordered locals not to aid the VC. The villagers tried to keep farming, but both sides often punished them for helping the enemy. In 1968, US troops massacred My Lai residents, turning more Americans against the war.

Strategic hamlets

In the early 1960s, South Vietnam built fortified towns guarded by militia. These "strategic hamlets" were surrounded by fences and ditches. Villagers were moved in to keep them from the VC. The program ended after a few years.

Dwellings

Coming close

A helicopter drops low to investigate villagers tending buffalo. ARVN troops are in the background. Locals never knew whether soldiers would think they were VC and fire on them. Life in a combat zone was dangerous.

After action

ARVN soldiers talk with villagers, having just fought off a VC ambush, in which an ARVN lieutenant was killed. His body lies in the bottom of the boat. If the soldiers think the locals helped the VC, their huts will likely be burned.

On trial

A "people's court" led by the VC tries a youth accused of aiding the ARVN. He was found guilty and sentenced to two years in prison. A companion was sentenced to death.

Rings of bamboo walls

The Pacification Program

This relief program aimed to "win hearts and minds" by bringing food and humanitarian aid. Here, a US chaplain shows Vietnamese children a toy trumpet.

Searching for Communists

Air Cavalry troopers search a house for NVA or VC soldiers in the Highlands, where NVA troops operated. Their agents could be among the civilians.

Shoulder basket

Chores in a war zone

Local women carrying shoulder baskets meet US Marines assembling on a road. The women keep to the middle as the troops part to let them pass.

Massacre at My Lai

Army Americal Division troops entered My Lai on March 16, 1968, looking for enemy soldiers. Believing the villagers supported the VC, they shot more than 300 men, women, and children. A cover-up followed, and only one officer, Lt. William L. Calley Jr., was ever convicted.

Fire and death

After killing civilians, the soldiers burned My Lai. There were no reports of troops being attacked. A year later, an ex-soldier wrote to President Nixon, the Pentagon, and members of Congress about the atrocity. Many Americans were outraged, and the antiwar movement gained strength.

Calley to court

William Calley, center, and his attorneys arrive for a pretrial hearing in Fort Benning, Georgia, in January 1970. Calley was sentenced to life in prison, but Nixon had this reduced to 20 years and later granted Calley parole; he spent just three days in a military jail.

Tunnels

The Vietnamese dug tunnels in the First Indochina War and continued to do so in Communist-controlled areas of South Vietnam during the Vietnam War. Guerrillas lived in the tunnels, which had bedrooms, kitchens, munitions depots, and hospitals. When US or Allied troops passed by, fighters hid in the tunnels or made surprise attacks.

Viet Cong tunnels

Vietnamese laborers use simple tools to dig a tunnel entrance, and baskets to remove dirt. This part of the tunnel will be hidden from view.

Wooden plug

Shrapnel pieces

VC antipersonnel mine

Trigger mechanism

Chinese cobra

Booby traps

The VC set traps to injure enemy troops coming into tunnel systems. Traps included mines detonated by trip wires and even venomous snakes, such as vipers or cobras.

Cu Chi

Cu Chi, the largest complex—with 155 miles (250 km) of tunnels—was 45 miles (72 km) north of Saigon. As this image from the Cu Chi Museum shows, complexes had electricity, air shafts, and an underwater entry.

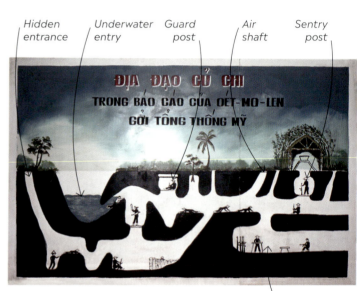

Hidden entrance *Underwater entry* *Guard post* *Air shaft* *Sentry post*

ĐỊA ĐẠO CỦ CHI
TRONG BÁO CÁO CỦA OET-MO-LEN
GỞI TỔNG THỐNG MỸ

Meeting room

Cover keeps out bugs and rodents

SKS Simonov carbine

On guard

A VC sentry waiting underground is alert for possible enemy discovery of his tunnel. The entrance to the tunnel is on the right.

Rice cooker

Wood stove

Wash bucket

Underground kitchen

Tunnel kitchens had vents that sent smoke in many directions so it wasn't seen above ground. Some VC lived underground for months. They emerged for quick attacks and just as suddenly vanished into the tunnels.

Flak jacket

Gas mask

Flashlight

Tunnel rats

"Tunnel rats" were a special breed of soldier who took on one of the most dangerous, frightening wartime duties. Armed with a pistol, knife, and flashlight, they crawled into dark, twisting VC tunnels to see if they led to a major complex. Inside there might be a VC sentry, a booby trap—or nothing at all.

Pull-ring

Strap

Tear gas mask

GAS
CN-DM

PB-2-68

Tear gas

Air filter

Gas and gas mask

Before entering a tunnel, a tunnel rat would toss in a tear-gas canister to force away guards. Wearing a gas mask, he then crawled inside.

Returning tunnel rat

A US soldier is pulled from a tunnel he searched. Americans were generally larger than Vietnamese and had trouble with the narrow passages. This man wears a gas mask against the tear gas he threw into the tunnel.

.45 caliber bullet

Special non-rolling design

Belt clip

Tunnel gear

The .45 pistol was the tunnel rat's most potent weapon, but he also carried a "Ka-Bar" combat knife. Sometimes, soldiers encountered enemies in the tunnels, and deadly shootouts resulted.

.45 pistol

Bullet and magazine

Flashlight

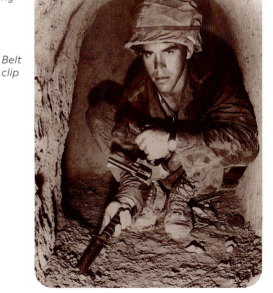

Tight fit

A 173rd Airborne Division engineer squats in a tunnel in the "Iron Triangle," a VC stronghold north of Saigon. His unit is searching for VC caches of ammo.

Handle

Hilt

Ka-Bar knife

Ka-Bar sheath

Tet Offensive

On January 21, 1968, the Communists ambushed a Marine base at Khe Sanh. Hanoi's offensive then erupted in South Vietnam on January 30, during the Vietnamese New Year, or "Tet." In four weeks, the Tet Offensive hit 100 cities and towns. The Communists lost, but the US knew the war would drag on.

Bases and government buildings in South Vietnam faced fierce assaults, particularly in Hué and Saigon.

The president studies Khe Sanh

LBJ and advisers examine a model of Khe Sanh. He believed Giap wanted to turn the siege into another Dien Bien Phu, forcing the US to withdraw, like the French in 1954.

Khe Sanh

Khe Sanh's 6,000 Marines and ARVN troops blocked enemy supply routes from Laos. The Communist siege of early 1968 drew Allied forces from the cities, which were soon attacked. Thousands of US and Allied troops battled to reach the base, which held out for 77 days until relief arrived.

Khe Sanh artillery

US gunners return enemy artillery fire. Every week, US and Allied troops were hit with 2,500 rounds of artillery, mortars, and rockets as they fought off infantry attacks.

Explosion at Khe Sanh

Marines duck as a munitions store is hit. Enemy gun positions filled the hills around Khe Sanh, but the US had overwhelming air power. Helicopter pilots flew supplies in and wounded men out. The siege ended on April 8 after US relief forces broke through.

Saigon

The main struggle of Tet was for Saigon; 19 VC fighters broke into the US embassy and fought for hours. Under General Weyand, US and Allied forces defended MACV's airfield headquarters.

Saigon recovers
Saigon had seen little violence before Tet. Afterward, residents had to pick their way through rubble to search for victims and clean up their homes.

Frederick C. Weyand
Commanding II Field Force (which defended Saigon), General Weyand pulled his forces nearer to Saigon. His success earned him overall command in Vietnam.

ARVN retakes Citadel
South Vietnamese troops plant their flag on Hué's shattered Citadel. US and ARVN forces attacked VC and NVA fighters at the fortress.

South Vietnamese flag

Hué

The battle for Hué ended on March 2. Fighting destroyed much of Hué and its ancient Imperial Citadel. The Communists lost Tet, but they won political victory: more Americans now opposed the war. After the turning point of Tet, the war increasingly favored the Communists.

👁 EYEWITNESS

Hoang Thi No
North Vietnamese spy Hoang Thi No was a member of the all-women Perfume River Squad—11 teenagers deployed to Hué from 1967. They played key roles in the Tet Offensive, organizing locals in advance, gathering information, and guiding Communist forces in the city.

After the battle
Members of the US Fifth Marine Regiment patrol a war-torn street in Hué. These troops reinforced Allied units and fought for three brutal weeks to recapture the city. The destroyed Imperial Citadel is in the background.

Antiwar movement

In 1965, with many Americans opposed to the war, 20,000 demonstrators marched in Washington, D.C. As the war widened, peaceful protests became angry. So troubled was President Johnson that he didn't stand for reelection in 1968. In 1970, college students were shot at protests in Ohio and Mississippi.

Voices for peace

Folk singer Joan Baez and musicians Pete Seeger, Bob Dylan, and the group Peter, Paul and Mary sang at protests.

 EYEWITNESS

Thich Nhat Hanh

A Buddhist monk and peace activist, Hanh (1926–2022) refused to take sides in the war. He was exiled from South Vietnam in 1966 and became a speaker, author, and spiritual leader. His Buddhist thought and practice applied spiritual values to modern issues.

Leaders

Famous doctor and author Benjamin Spock, left, with civil rights leader Dr. Martin Luther King, Jr. at a 5,000-strong antiwar rally in Chicago in 1967. The influence of such well-regarded leaders convinced many Americans to oppose the war.

moratorium

1969 Moratorium Against the War button

US Capitol Building

Flowers instead of bullets

In one of the most famous antiwar images, a demonstrator places carnations in the barrels of military police rifles. This incident took place in 1967, when more than 100,000 people protested at the Pentagon in Washington, D.C.

Fighting back

A protester in Berkeley, California, hurls a tear gas canister back at police who had fired it, in 1970. Tear gas forced most demonstrators to retreat.

Kent State

Ohio National Guardsmen fire tear gas at Kent State University protestors in May 1970. Troops later killed four students and wounded others—some just walking to class.

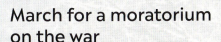

March for a moratorium on the war

In November 1969, huge demonstrations urged a temporary halt in the fighting. One march filled Pennsylvania Avenue, near the Capitol Building in Washington, D.C. Signs called for the withdrawal of US troops and the release of jailed activists.

Vietnam veterans against the war

Vietnam veterans, such as these marchers in Miami Beach in 1972, were among the most vocal antiwar activists. Many discarded their war medals in protest.

Silver Star

Dove of peace

McGovern campaign button

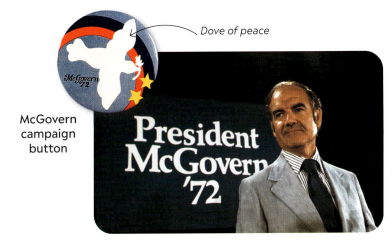

Peace candidate

Senator George McGovern of South Dakota ran unsuccessfully against Nixon in 1972. He was well-respected, but could not unify Democrats behind his antiwar message.

51

US withdraws

In 1969, President Nixon pressed for "Vietnamization" of the war—training South Vietnam's forces to take on a larger role and withdrawing US forces, which numbered 543,000. But many top ARVN officers lacked military ability. It would take years to replace US troops, and bloody battles with American casualties continued even as the US was leaving.

Homeward bound

Troops board a Chinook en route to the US. Withdrawal of 25,000 US troops began in June 1969.

A victory

South Vietnamese security forces fighting alongside the ARVN show off a captured North Vietnamese flag. Viet Cong arms and munitions were taken during counterinsurgency operations near the DMZ.

North Vietnamese flag

RVN flag

Creighton Abrams

General Abrams took command of MACV in 1968, replacing General Westmoreland. Abrams was ordered to end large-scale US operations and supervise Vietnamization of the war.

A chest full of medals

South Vietnamese president Thieu awards a medal, joined by General Lam Quang Thi. These two led the Vietnamization effort, but Thieu was criticized as a weak military leader.

General Thi   President Thieu

AVRN troops on patrol

South Vietnamese Marines gather at a Mekong Delta village to cut a VC supply route. As US troops withdrew, the ARVN began drafting men aged 17 to 43.

Hamburger Hill

On May 10, 1969, heliborne troops attacked NVA forces dug in on Ap Bia Mountain, near the Laos border. After 10 days, there were 46 US deaths and 400 wounded. Troopers dubbed it "Hamburger Hill," feeling it was a meat grinder. With ARVN troops, they captured Ap Bia, but were then told to abandon it. Many felt the losses in this last major US battle had been for nothing.

Yellow Leopard patch

Black Dragon patch

Patches

South Vietnamese Special Forces wore patches. Yellow Leopards were paratroopers. Black Dragons attacked the Ho Chi Minh Trail.

Reinforcements land

Paratroopers join the battle for Ap Bia. The peak dominated the strategic A Shau Valley, a route for VC troops and supplies to the Central Highlands.

Medics aid the wounded

US and ARVN "walking wounded" come down Ap Bia Mountain with the help of medics after Hamburger Hill—to be taken to rear units for treatment, flown out by medevac helicopters, or to return to their units.

Last air assaults

Through 1970, US forces withdrew, but air support continued. Nixon ordered bombings in Cambodia. By 1972, US offensive operations had ended: only 70,000 US troops remained. In February, Nixon opened talks with Chinese premier Zhou Enlai. In March 1972, Hanoi sent 125,000 troops on the attack. ARVN units fell back until the "Linebacker" air campaign struck strategic targets in the North. ARVN troops pushed back the Communists, ending the "Spring Offensive."

KEY BATTLES OF 1972

NORTH VIETNAM

CHINA

NVA bases and supply routes

DMZ

Quang Tri
Hué

LAOS

Kontum
Pleiku

CAMBODIA

SOUTH VIETNAM

Central Highlands

An Loc

Tay Ninh

Saigon

N W E S

Mekong River

South China Sea

✳ Battle sites ▬ NVA Eastertide Offensive
▬ Areas lost by South Vietnam in 1972

The NVA offensive of March 30 surprised the ARVN. The invasion triggered struggles at Kontum, Quang Tri, and An Loc. The Communists were defeated by September.

Advancing NVA soldiers

Camouflaged NVA troops trudge along a trail in Cambodia. They are heading for South Vietnam to join the Spring Offensive of 1972.

Preparing to fire

An NVA soldier loads a shell into a mortar—a favored Communist weapon. Most mortars could be carried by two soldiers.

Awaiting a lift

South Vietnamese troops near An Loc prepare for helicopter transport in April 1972. An Loc was between the Communists and their objective—Saigon, 75 miles (120 km) away.

> The 66-day Battle of An Loc was **a tactical victory** for South Vietnam.

James Hollingsworth

General James Hollingsworth planned air attacks at An Loc and advised ARVN corps defending Saigon.

Loading bombs

USS *Constellation* crew load fighter-bombers with 500-lb (230-kg) bombs for the Linebacker campaign, which also mined North Vietnamese harbors to disrupt supplies for Hanoi's war effort.

Cobra helicopter

Cobra attack helicopters such as this Air Cav gunship were highly effective weapons during Linebacker. Over 200 Soviet-made tanks led the Spring Offensive, but were no match for the Cobras.

Rockets could destroy tanks.

Cobra helicopter crewman's patch

Antitank weapon

The shoulder-fired LAW (light antitank weapon) was key in the ARVN's battle with NVA tanks. Its 66-mm rockets could knock out Soviet-made armor.

ARVN counterattack

ARVN tanks breach NVA lines during their counterthrust at Quang Tri. US air superiority meant tank crews did not worry about attacks from above. Led by General Ngo Quang Truong, its most capable general, the ARVN recaptured the province.

Air force patch

This patch marks Operation Bullet Shot (1972). Dozens of US B-52 bombers flew from Guam to attack North Vietnam.

The Christmas Bombing

In October 1972, Nixon called off the air war when it looked as though there would be a breakthrough in peace talks in Paris, France. But when these broke down, Nixon restarted air strikes. Operation Linebacker II, from December 18 to 30, was the heaviest bombing attack of the entire war. The "Christmas Bombing" campaign targeted North Vietnamese industry and transportation, and brought all parties back to the table to sign a ceasefire.

Heroism

Distinguished Flying Cross (DFC) medals are awarded for heroism in flight, in combat or noncombat. Two were awarded in Linebacker II.

Weaving leaves and brush together

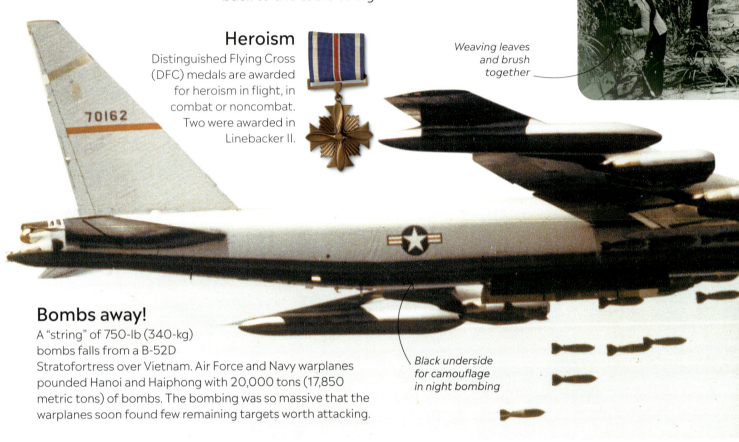

Bombs away!

A "string" of 750-lb (340-kg) bombs falls from a B-52D Stratofortress over Vietnam. Air Force and Navy warplanes pounded Hanoi and Haiphong with 20,000 tons (17,850 metric tons) of bombs. The bombing was so massive that the warplanes soon found few remaining targets worth attacking.

Black underside for camouflage in night bombing

US aircraft down

North Vietnamese women salvage parts from the wreckage of an F-111. In Linebacker II, the Air Force lost 20 planes (plus a helicopter); the Navy lost six.

Antiaircraft defenses

North Vietnamese militia load an antiaircraft gun. The US lost 26 planes in Linebacker II, including 15 B-52s. Artillery and MiG fighters took three each, SAMs downed 17, and three crashed. Even so, Linebacker II ruined northern air defenses.

Continued from previous page

Palm leaves

Concealing a bridge

North Vietnamese villagers camouflage a bridge with foliage—air attacks targeted bridges to cut transport links. Camouflage protected small bridges that were essential to the movement of people, but large bridges were easy targets.

Camouflage

Clearing wood debris

Xuan Thuy

The DRV's chief public negotiator in Paris was a formidable spokesperson. Hanoi's leaders, Secretary Le Duan and key adviser Le Duc Tho, were willing to let the talks collapse if the terms were unsatisfactory.

Hospital in ruins

Searching for supplies, medics pick through the rubble of a Hanoi hospital destroyed by the Christmas Bombing. US airmen tried to avoid hospitals and schools, but high-altitude bombing was not accurate.

AIR FORCE

Paris Peace Accords

On January 27, 1973, the United States, North Vietnam, South Vietnam, and the Viet Cong signed the Paris Peace Accords. These provided for a ceasefire and a US withdrawal. Le Duc Tho and Henry Kissinger won the Nobel Prize for Peace in 1973, but Tho refused it. His reluctance was vindicated when the war did not end until 1975.

Discussing peace terms

Delegates sat in a circle, so no one was "head of the table" and symbolically in charge. A ceasefire was signed on January 27, 1973. Secretary of State William Rogers signed for the US.

Henry Kissinger   *Le Duc Tho*

Delegates

Henry Kissinger talks with Le Duc Tho through an interpreter. Although official peace talks began in 1972, secret discussions had started between the two sides two to three years earlier.

👁 **EYEWITNESS**

Nguyễn Thị Bình
Viet Cong head diplomat "Madame Bình" was the face of the NLF in Paris and the only woman to sign the Paris Accords. After reunification, she became a minister and later Vice President of Vietnam.

Prisoners of war

More than 660 US personnel were taken prisoner of war (POW) and held in camps in North Vietnam, South Vietnam, Laos, and Cambodia. Communist prisoners went to ARVN camps. All POWs were set for release with the US withdrawal. In 1973, Operation Homecoming took US POWs home. Some 1,600 men remained missing in action (MIA).

Parade of prisoners
American POWs are marched under guard through Hanoi in 1966. Most US POWs were downed Air Force or Navy airmen—30 escaped.

POW/MIA bracelet
As a remembrance, Americans wore silver bracelets inscribed with the names of POWs or MIAs and the dates of their capture or disappearance.

Nurse Patricia Anderson

EYEWITNESS

Sybil Stockdale
An advocate for American prisoners of war, Sybil Stockdale (1924–2015), left, founded the National League of POW/MIA Families in 1966. She drew public attention to the torture of POWs by North Vietnam and asked the government to intervene.

A nurse's comfort
Nurse Lt. Patricia Anderson wore a bracelet for Lt. Charles Norris. Upon his release, she helped nurse him back to health.

POW medal

First freedom
American POWs under North Vietnamese guard disembark from a bus on their way to a Hanoi airport in 1973. Their release was arranged as part of the Paris peace talks.

Communist POWs

There is no accurate count of the thousands of Communist fighters and sympathizers imprisoned during the war. NVA and VC captives went to POW camps in South Vietnam. They were usually interrogated, often brutally—especially by the ARVN. The peace agreement arranged for POW exchanges between the Communists and US.

Former NVA POW

The Communists honored their own POWs. Nguyen Huu Thanh, a former US captive, wears the NVA's POW medal.

NVA POW medal

Communist star

Hands breaking free from chains

POW medal

Victory medal

Dreary accommodations

American POWs at the "Hanoi Hilton," as they called their prison, have been allowed to talk between bars.

A survivor and captive

An NVA soldier of the 304th Division sits, bound and battle-shocked, under the eye of a trooper from the 1st Air Cavalry Division. He was taken during fighting at Ia Drang Valley.

Joyful welcome

Air Force colonel Robert Stirm rushes to embrace his family at Travis Air Force Base, March 1973. He was a POW for more than five years.

Taking in captives

Suspected Viet Cong are brought in for interrogation. The youthfulness of the captives was typical of many South Vietnamese, who seemed to be farmers, but were actually guerrillas.

59

The fall of Saigon

By 1974, Congress had cut off funds to aid Saigon. When the NVA invaded Phuoc Long later that year, the South Vietnamese were on their own. Better armed than the ARVN, the NVA swept through South Vietnam from March 1975, capturing Saigon in April to end 30 years of fighting.

Van Tien Dung

NVA Chief of Staff since 1953, General Dung took overall command to plan and lead the campaign that broke ARVN lines in the Central Highlands and took Saigon.

Looking for safety

ARVN soldiers help villagers cross a footbridge 50 miles (80 km) outside Saigon. Frightened South Vietnamese left their homes to escape the fighting. Many had no food, water, or shelter. Thousands died.

400 people were left in the US Embassy compound.

FINAL CAMPAIGN

DMZ
Hué
LAOS
Da Nang
SOUTH VIETNAM
CAMBODIA
Central Highlands
Ban Me Thuot
Phuoc Long
Phnom Penh
Cam Ranh Bay
Xuan Loc
Saigon
Mekong River
N W E S
South China Sea

━━━ Final NVA campaign March–April 1975
★ South Vietnamese cities and provinces captured by the NVA

The NVA offensive of March–April 1975 was named the Ho Chi Minh Campaign. ARVN troops fought hard, even though they were attacked from all sides and had no US air support. The ARVN inflicted heavy casualties on the NVA, but were wiped out in less than two months.

The struggle to escape

Saigon citizens waving ID papers try to board a US Embassy airport bus. Many were government or American employees fearful of Communist reprisals.

Last-minute evacuation

A US helicopter loads passengers near the US Embassy on April 29, 1975. By April 30, when South Vietnam surrendered, more than 3,000 Americans, South Vietnamese, and others had been evacuated.

Crashing the palace gates

A tank sporting a Viet Cong flag rumbles into the South Vietnamese presidential palace compound on the day of surrender. Until now, infantry and guerrillas had done most of the Communist fighting, but the final offensive was modern, mechanized, and spearheaded by NVA armor.

The wake of defeat

Afraid of capture, thousands of ARVN soldiers threw away their uniforms and boots as they tried to escape Saigon on April 30. This photo was taken by Communists entering the city.

Victory medal

The Victory Order and Decoration was awarded for fighting South Vietnam, the US, and their allies. It had also been given for fighting the French.

Rejoicing in Hanoi

Marchers carry signs, banners, and pictures of Ho Chi Minh. Military units join the celebration, which marked the end of a century-long struggle for independence.

Aftermath

More than 58,000 Americans died in the war and 153,000 were wounded; 1 million Vietnamese combatants and 4 million civilians died. The new Socialist Republic of Vietnam was a nation shattered by war. Many tried to escape. Today, the population is 101 million (up from 49 million in 1976) and 60 percent of the population live in cities. Economic growth is a healthy 5 percent.

Nationalist poster
Hanoi became Vietnam's capital. Saigon was renamed Ho Chi Minh City. This 1980 poster shows the dove of peace over a united nation.

Buddhism
Both South Vietnam and the Communist victors repressed Buddhism, seeing it as a threat to political unity. Many Buddhists protested against the war, calling for compassion to heal the country.

Remembering the fallen
Visitors to a cemetery honor fallen NVA soldiers at the Vietnamese New Year by burning incense beside the graves. ARVN cemeteries, however, are usually neglected.

A time of peace
Newlyweds pose before a statue of Ho in Ho Chi Minh City. With 9.5 million inhabitants, it is Vietnam's largest city.

Life goes on
A farmer's elephant lumbers by a rusting tank more than 10 years after the war. Vietnam had an enormous task clearing away ruined military equipment after the conflict

The boat people

As Saigon fell, modern history's largest flight of refugees by sea began. South Vietnam's "boat people" fled in small, overcrowded vessels. Many drowned. Some families spent their life savings to send their children off in a boat. More than 1 million refugees from the conflict settled in the US.

This overloaded vessel is dangerously low in the water.

Rescued

These boat people have been rescued in the South China Sea. Most are ex-government officials or soldiers and their families. The next waves of refugees would be farmers and laborers.

In Hong Kong harbor

In 1979, 69,000 boat people such as those shown above made the 1,000-mile (1,600-km) voyage to Hong Kong. Many were Amerasians—children of Vietnamese women and US soldiers.

Vietnam veterans

Many people accused veterans of having lost the conflict or fighting an unjust war. At first, some US veterans' groups did not want Vietnam vets as members. Eventually, it became clear how well Allied troops had done their duty, and they were given the respect they had earned.

Fuse (or trigger)

Land mines

Thousands of mines like this Soviet antitank landmine remain in Vietnam. More than 40,000 Vietnamese have been killed by uncleared mines.

Veteran's buckle

This belt buckle shows Australian service in the war.

Written in stone

A Vietnam vet touches "The Wall," a memorial in Washington, D.C., bearing the names of over 58,000 US war dead. It opened in 1982.

US veterans

Vietnam veterans parade past saluting spectators during 1993 Veterans Day events at the Vietnam Veterans Memorial. Around 1.6 million US personnel fought or were exposed to attacks in Vietnam.

Did you know?

AMAZING FACTS

One-third of the top National Liberation Front (NLF) political officers were women. Among the most important was Nguyễn Thị Bình, chief NLF representative at the Paris peace talks. Many entered the Vietnamese government after the war.

"Mining" warplanes for metals was profitable. The instruments of a US warplane contained up to $5,000 worth of gold, silver, and platinum.

US soldiers often painted their vehicles with an "Ace Of Death" playing card symbol, considered bad luck in Vietnam. They used it to frighten superstitious Vietnamese.

US soldiers were told to destroy letters they received. So, if a soldier were captured, the enemy would not be able to find out personal information from the letters. Most troops kept their letters, however, and reread them often.

Death's Head playing card

NVA field officers wore no badge of rank. They carried pens to show they were officers. The pen was secured with a string and kept in a shirt pocket.

North Vietnamese officer's pen

In the early 1970s, the ARVN captured so many AK-47 assault rifles from the NVA that they gave away thousands to other Southeast Asian armies.

Documents circulated secretly among Communist commanders and officials in South Vietnam were stamped with coded symbols.

An estimated 50,000 Vietnamese children were fathered by US soldiers. The men returned home, leaving mothers and children behind. These "Amerasians" were discriminated against by the Vietnamese government, which considered them American. Some were adopted in the US; most remained outcasts in Vietnam.

The $8.4 million collected to erect the Vietnam Veterans Memorial included donations from more than 275,000 people.

French author Bernard Fall was the leading authority on the Indochina conflict. US commander William Westmoreland studied his works. A former French soldier, Fall attended college in the US and became a professor at Howard University. His works, such as *Street Without Joy*, chronicled the First Indochina War. He was killed by a mine in Vietnam in 1967.

Soldiers on patrol did not use anything with a fragrance, such as soap or cologne. The VC might detect the odor and know they were nearby.

Of the 7,484 US women who served in Vietnam, 6,250 (83.5 percent) were nurses. Ten women from the military died, as did 56 civilians—including missionaries, nurses, and journalists. In one tragedy, 37 civilian women died in a plane crash while escorting Amerasian orphans out of the country in April 1975.

NVA stamp for official documents

Just as US troops had performers entertain them, NVA and VC troops had their own entertainers. Some performances were given in theater spaces in tunnels.

These girls, seen in Ho Chi Minh City, have Vietnamese mothers and American fathers.

Performers entertain North Vietnamese troops.

QUESTIONS AND ANSWERS

H-21 Shawnee transport helicopter

Montagnards sometimes gave US soldiers friendship bracelets and flutes.

Were any Vietnamese ethnic groups US allies?

Yes, many Montagnards, or "mountain peoples" (now called Dega), aided the US and some fought on until 1992. The Hmong were also allies. Thousands from both groups fled Vietnam after the war.

What is a flash grenade?

It is a nonlethal hand grenade. Its flash and bang confuse the enemy, who can then be captured.

What was the deadliest year of the war?

More combat deaths occurred in 1968 than any other year. This is the case for all of the main fighting forces, including US, ARVN, NVA, and VC troops, with losses up to 70,000.

Had major wars been fought in Vietnam before the 20th century?

The Vietnamese battled five Chinese invasions after 939CE. They defeated Kublai Khan three times—the last in 1287, routing 300,000 Mongol invaders. China recognized Vietnam's independence in 1427.

What is a "flying banana"?

This was the nickname given to banana-shaped military transport helicopters. The H-21 Shawnee has rotors "in tandem"—at the front and back.

What is the US K-9 Corps?

The K-9 (for canine) Corps trains dogs for military duties. German shepherds were used as sentry dogs, to sniff out booby traps, and to find VC tunnels. They were so valuable that enemy mortars targeted dog shelters.

What was the "domino theory"?

The theory was that if South Vietnam fell to the Communists, then other Southeast Asian nations would fall too—just as a row of dominoes can knock each other down.

When is the worst weather in Vietnam?

Monsoon season—in summer or winter—has endless rain. Soldiers' clothing never dried, causing boils, disease, and parasite infections.

Flash grenade

How educated were US soldiers?

The average nonofficer was educated up to the age of 19: one year of college. Among volunteers, 79 percent had a high school diploma.

Where was the fiercest fighting?

Near South Vietnam's borders with the North and Laos—53 percent of Americans killed died in four provinces: Quang Tri, Thua Thien, Quang Nam, and Quan Tin.

What was the main air force target in the North?

The Doumer Bridge, which carried trains coming from the north into Hanoi. Freight moving by rail from China and the seaport of Haiphong crossed this bridge.

K-9 unit soldier

Did Buddhist monks oppose the war?

Yes, they called for negotiations between the Allied forces and the Communists. Monks praying in the streets for peace were oppressed by government troops.

South Vietnamese Buddhist monks are penned in by barbed wire as they demonstrate in the early 1970s.

Timeline

In 1946, Vietnamese Communists in Indochina rose up against the French. This First Indochina War ended in defeat of the US-backed French. Vietnam was divided into the Communist North and capitalist South. For 20 years, the US supported the South. The Second Indochina War—the Vietnam War—cost the lives of 58,000 Americans, 1 million Vietnamese combatants, and 4 million civilians. In 1973, US troops withdrew. South Vietnam fell two years later.

Destroyer USS *Maddox* in Gulf of Tonkin

1945-1946 INDOCHINA STRUGGLE

In August 1945, Japan surrenders in World War II, giving up control of French colonies in Indochina. Vietnamese Communist Ho Chi Minh declares the independent Democratic Republic of Vietnam (DRV). France sends troops. First Indochina War begins.

1950-1953 START OF US ADVISORY PHASE

US Military Assistance Advisory Group (MAAG) is set up to aid the French against the Vietminh, the rebel army. The US helps fund the French. The insurgents win control of the countryside.

1954 TWO VIETNAMS

The fall in May 1954 of Dien Bien Phu, a French base in northern Indochina, ends the First Indochina War. Peace terms divide the country temporarily into the Vietminh-controlled DRV in the North and the Republic of Vietnam (RVN) in the South. The Vietnamese are to vote on their form of government.

1955-1963 ARMED REVOLT

In 1955, Ngo Dinh Diem becomes president of South Vietnam, and will not allow a vote. Armed insurrection resumes, with the DRV supporting rebels known as Viet Cong (VC). US military advisers increase to 16,000 by 1963, when the Army of the Republic of Vietnam (ARVN) is defeated at Ap Bac.

1963 ASSASSINATIONS

On November 2, a US-backed military coup in South Vietnam overthrows and assassinates Diem. US President John F. Kennedy is assassinated on November 22; he is succeeded by Vice President Lyndon B. Johnson.

1964 GULF OF TONKIN INCIDENT

In August, the US military alleges that North Vietnamese gunboats attacked a US vessel in the Gulf of Tonkin. The Senate passes the Gulf of Tonkin Resolution, giving LBJ broad war powers. Air strikes begin on the North.

1965 DIRECT US INTERVENTION

February-March VC attack US base at Pleiku. Marine combat troops are deployed to Vietnam and Operation Rolling Thunder begins. LBJ increases US forces to 33,000 troops.

June-July Battle at Dong Xoai pits US and ARVN forces against VC guerrillas. LBJ commits 125,000 troops.

Eisenhower, center, welcomes Ngo Dinh Diem, front left, at Washington National Airport, 1957.

August Operation Starlite, first major US ground offensive starts; Operation Market Time attacks enemy seaborne supply routes to South Vietnam.

November Battle of Ia Drang Valley involves Air Cavalry assault, first major engagement by troops carried into battle and resupplied by helicopter. Pentagon calls for 400,000 troops.

1966 AIR AND GROUND WARFARE

January After a pause in bombing North Vietnam (in a failed attempt at negotiations), LBJ resumes US air campaign.

March VC and North Vietnamese Army troops attack and destroy US Special Forces base in A Shau Valley.

June Massive US air raids on Hanoi and Haiphong destroy much of North Vietnam's fuel supplies.

August Australian troops win Battle of Long Tan.

September-November Operation Attleboro drives VC forces across Cambodian border.

1967 WAR AND ANTIWAR

January Operation Bolo: air campaign inflicts heavy losses on North Vietnamese; in Operation Cedar Falls, US and ARVN troops attack the VC-controlled "Iron Triangle" near Saigon.

February In Operation Junction City, US and ARVN strike enemy bases north of Saigon.

April Major antiwar demonstrations in New York City and San Francisco indicate US public is not fully behind war.

May Secretary of Defense Robert McNamara decides war policy is not working; recommends cutting back on bombing. LBJ unsure of course to follow.

July Marines battle NVA at Con Thien; McNamara visits Saigon, and agrees to add 55,000 troops.

August US bombing campaign against North intensifies.

October Antiwar march by 50,000 on Washington, D.C.; bombing of Hanoi and Haiphong increases.

November–December Battle of Dak To

1968 DEPTHS OF WAR

January– February Massive NVA-VC offensive during the Buddhist New Year, called Tet. South Vietnam is aflame for weeks before the US and government forces regain control.

President Johnson consults with Secretary of Defense Robert McNamara in February 1968.

January–April Siege of US base at Khe Sanh; Marines fight off NVA and hold out until siege is broken. Clark Clifford replaces McNamara as Secretary of Defense.

March My Lai Massacre: US troops of the American Division kill more than 300 civilians at the RVN hamlet of My Lai. Disheartened by growing opposition to the war, and his health failing, LBJ declares he will not run again for president.

July Phoenix program begins: secret campaign to kill enemy sympathizers allegedly kills 40,000 South Vietnamese.

October Rolling Thunder ends. In Rolling Thunder, more bombs were dropped on North Vietnam than the US used in the Pacific Theater in World War II.

November Richard Nixon is elected president, promising to bring peace with honor.

1969 PEACE DISCUSSIONS

January First meetings held in Paris for peace talks. Marines in Operation Dewey Canyon find enemy supply roads from Laos.

March Operation Menu: Nixon approves secret bombing campaign in Cambodia. Policy of Vietnamization begins.

ARVN troops recapture the Citadel at Hué, during Tet Offensive.

May 101st Airborne troops capture Hill 937 in the "Battle of Hamburger Hill," costing 46 US lives. It is soon abandoned.

June Nixon announces withdrawal of 25,000 troops later in the year. Regular troop reductions will continue.

August Henry Kissinger meets with North Vietnamese representative in Paris.

September Ho Chi Minh dies at age 79.

1970 WIDENING WAR

April–May US troops invade Cambodia to attack Communist positions.

May Ohio National Guard fires on antiwar demonstrators at Kent State University, killing four and wounding 10.

June Senate repeals Gulf of Tonkin Resolution.

1971 VIETNAMIZATION

February–April ARVN troops strike in Laos in Operation Lam Son.

November US troops number 139,000, down from a peak of 543,500.

1972 BOMBS SPUR TALKS

February Nixon visits China, meets Mao Zedong and other leaders.

March–July NVA opens new offensives.

May–October Nixon orders Operation Linebacker, a massive bombing campaign against North Vietnam.

December Communist negotiators hesitate to make peace, so Operation Linebacker II renews bombing.

1973–1975 COMMUNIST TRIUMPH

January 1973 Paris Peace Accords signed by US, North Vietnam, South Vietnam, and Viet Cong; US military presence in Vietnam ends 60 days later.

August 1974 Nixon resigns in disgrace after the Watergate scandal. Vice President Gerald Ford becomes president and pardons Nixon.

January 1975 North Vietnam intensifies military campaign against South Vietnam.

March–April 1975 Communist offensive captures Saigon on April 30. North and South Vietnam are united as the Socialist Republic of Vietnam. Hanoi is the capital.

US troops board a helicopter to return home in 1969.

Find out **more**

The story of the Indochina conflict is told at museums, libraries, and war memorials. Memorials are places where people can honor those who served. Major memorials are in the United States, Vietnam, Australia, South Korea, and France.

Memorial in Australia

The Australian Vietnam Forces National Memorial in Canberra was dedicated in 1992. Its concrete forms are inspired by ancient sacred sites built of "standing stones."

A national tribute

The Vietnam Veterans Memorial in Washington, D.C., honors Americans who served in Vietnam. "The Wall," engraved with the names of the fallen, is the centerpiece. Below are some of the monuments it contains.

Vietnam Women's Memorial

This sculpture pays tribute to the women who served. Dedicated in 1993, it shows nurses tending a wounded soldier. One looks upward for help—from a chopper, or a higher power?

Three Servicemen

Frederick Hart designed this 1984 memorial, which portrays soldiers in the field.

A rubbing

Visitors can place paper against a name and create a rubbing. Ceremonies are held at the site on Memorial Day and Veterans Day.

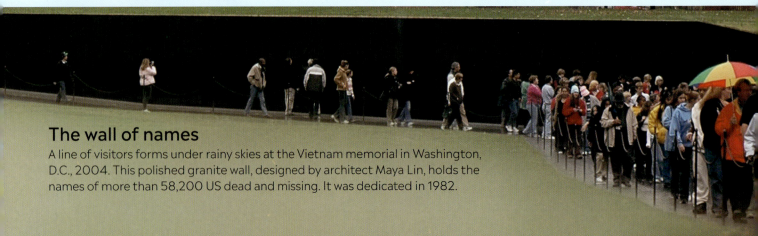

The wall of names

A line of visitors forms under rainy skies at the Vietnam memorial in Washington, D.C., 2004. This polished granite wall, designed by architect Maya Lin, holds the names of more than 58,200 US dead and missing. It was dedicated in 1982.

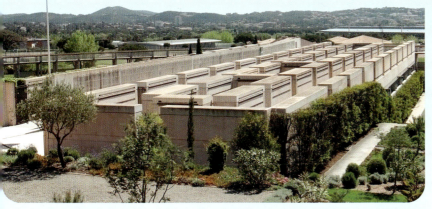

Memorial in France

The Memorial to the Wars in Indochina honors French veterans. Opened in Fréjus in 1993, it holds the remains of more than 23,000 citizens—including 3,515 civilians—who died from 1940 to 1954.

Australia's war museum

The Australian War Memorial, Canberra, pays tribute to the dead from all the nation's wars. The museum uses exhibits and research facilities to teach about war.

Tunnel tours

The former VC tunnel complex at Cu Chi is one of Vietnam's most popular tourist attractions. Visitors go into the tunnels to see reconstructed living spaces, including barracks, meeting rooms, and kitchens.

Learning about the war

Vietnamese schoolchildren take a class trip to view a MiG-21 fighter at a Hanoi military museum. This plane was in the squadron that defended their city against US air raids. The trip is part of a 25th-anniversary celebration of the fall of Saigon.

PLACES TO VISIT

NATIONAL MUSEUM OF AMERICAN HISTORY, WASHINGTON, D.C.
"The Price of Freedom: Americans At War" exhibit examines the ways war has shaped US history. It features the Vietnam War.

NATIONAL MUSEUM OF THE US AIR FORCE, DAYTON, OHIO
This is the world's largest military aviation museum. Exhibits include US helicopters and fixed-wing aircraft of the Vietnam War.

NEW YORK VIETNAM VETERANS MEMORIAL, NEW YORK, NEW YORK
Excerpts of letters, diary entries, and poems written by Americans during the war are etched into the Memorial wall. These are supplemented by news dispatches.

VIETNAM-ERA EDUCATION CENTER, NEW JERSEY VIETNAM VETERANS' MEMORIAL, HOLMDEL, NEW JERSEY
The first museum of its kind in the US, the center focuses solely on the Vietnam War. The collection includes photos, timelines, films, letters, and interactive displays.

THE IMPERIAL CITADEL, HUÉ, VIETNAM
The Citadel in Hué was the residence of the Nguyen emperors. Much of the Citadel was reduced to rubble in the Tet Offensive of 1968, but key buildings have been restored.

WEST POINT MUSEUM, WEST POINT, NEW YORK
The galleries interpret the history of the US Army from colonial times to today. Weapons, gear, and art are shown in displays devoted to the Vietnam War. An NVA uniform is shown along with US jungle fatigues.

USEFUL WEBSITES

- Read about The Vietnam Project at Texas Tech University:
  www.vietnam.ttu.edu
- View photographs that show a North Vietnamese perspective:
  www.anothervietnam.com
- This National Park Service site details the building of the Vietnam Veterans Memorial:
  www.nps.gov/vive
- Learn about the thousands of women who served during the Vietnam War, including firsthand accounts:
  www.vietnamwomensmemorial.org
- Learn more about the Mobile Riverine Force:
  www.mrfa.org

Glossary

COBRA AH-1G attack helicopter

AGENT ORANGE Toxic chemical used by the US military to kill vegetation. Many Vietnam vets and Vietnamese suffered health problems from Agent Orange. Its name came from the orange stripe on its containers.

AIRBORNE Soldiers who are trained parachutists, also called paratroopers. In Vietnam, helicopters usually carried these troops into battle.

AIR CAVALRY The helicopter-borne infantry "Air Cav" was supported by fire from helicopter gunships; many Air Cav troopers were part of former horse cavalry regiments.

AIRMOBILE Helicopter-borne (heliborne) infantry whose units and tactics were first developed during the Vietnam War.

AK–47 assault rifle

AK-47 Soviet-manufactured Kalashnikov assault rifle that was a favored weapon of the VC and NVA.

ANTIAIRCRAFT GUN A gun with enough range to destroy enemy aircraft.

ARVN Acronym for the Army of the Republic of (South) Vietnam: the South Vietnamese regular army; pronounced "Arvin."

BASE CAMP A central resupply base for units in the field; location for headquarters, artillery batteries, and airfields.

BOAT PEOPLE South Vietnamese refugees who fled by boat after the Communist victory in 1975. Thousands drowned in the South China Sea. Many were rescued and taken in by neighboring countries and the US.

CHINOOK CH-47 A US cargo helicopter with two large rotors.

CHOPPER A helicopter. Vietnam was the first "helicopter war."

CLAYMORE Widely used antipersonnel mine that hurled projectiles up to 300 ft (100 m).

COBRA AH-1G attack helicopter, armed with rockets and machine guns.

COLONY A region or country politically controlled and occupied by a foreign nation.

COMMUNISM A political system in which property, such as land and factories, is owned by communities or the government.

COMPOUND A fortified US or Allied installation that served as a camp and fortress.

COUNTERINSURGENCY Organized antiguerrilla (anti-insurgent) warfare that armed and trained local militias to defend their communities. Methods included guerrilla tactics of surprise, concealment, and assassination.

DEFOLIATION Destroying vegetation (foliage) by spraying toxic chemicals such as Agent Orange. It was widely used in Vietnam.

DMZ The Demilitarized Zone was the dividing line between North and South Vietnam at the 17th parallel. It was to be kept free of military installations or occupation.

DRV Democratic Republic of Vietnam—the original name given by Ho Chi Minh to Vietnam when he proclaimed independence in 1945. After 1954, the name referred to Communist-dominated North Vietnam, with the capital Hanoi.

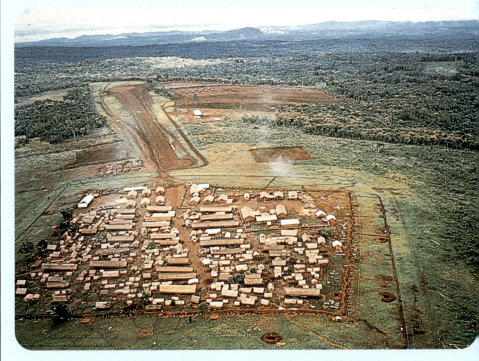
Special Forces base camp in the Central Highlands

Dustoff buckle

DUSTOFF Emergency evacuation of the wounded by a medical helicopter; a medevac.

FLAK JACKET A vest worn for protection from shrapnel—metal hurled by shells, mines, or grenades.

FRIENDLY FIRE Accidental attacks on US or Allied soldiers by other US or Allied soldiers, aircraft, or artillery—usually the result of being mistaken for the enemy.

FUSELAGE The body of an aircraft.

GREEN BERETS US Special Forces trained in counterinsurgency warfare and for operations behind enemy positions; they wore green berets.

GUERRILLA WARFARE A type of military attack in which independent groups of fighters that are not part of the regular armed forces participate.

GUNSHIP An armed helicopter or fixed-wing aircraft used to support ground troops.

HANOI HILTON Name of North Vietnam's Hoa Lo Prison given by Americans held prisoner there; Hiltons are famous luxury hotels.

HUEY Nickname for the UH-1 helicopters.

IN-COUNTRY A soldier serving in Vietnam was said to be "in-country."

INDOCHINA A historical European term for the peninsular region in Southeast Asia consisting of Myanmar, Thailand, Laos, Cambodia, Vietnam, and Malaysia.

IRON TRIANGLE Viet Cong-dominated area between the Thi Tinh and Saigon rivers northwest of Saigon.

LZ A landing zone for helicopters, usually near the battlefront. LZs often grew into permanent base camps.

M-16 American assault rifle used by US and ARVN troops.

MAAG Military Assistance Advisory Group, US military advisers sent to Vietnam.

MACV Military Assistance Command, Vietnam; it replaced MAAG in 1962.

MEDEVAC Evacuation of the wounded from the battlefield by helicopter.

MIA "Missing in Action," the military term for a serviceman or woman whose whereabouts after combat are unknown.

NAPALM A jellied petroleum material that burns fiercely; it is fired from flamethrowers or contained in bombs.

Flak jacket

NLF National Liberation Front, the political wing of the South Vietnamese insurgency fighting the Republic of (South) Vietnam.

NVA North Vietnamese Army—the regular troops of the DRV.

PARATROOPER An equipped soldier air-dropped into combat territory, wearing a parachute.

POW "Prisoner of War"—a serviceman or woman who has been captured by the enemy.

PUNJI STICKS Sharpened bamboo stakes set in camouflaged pits.

RVN Republic of Vietnam, the name given to South Vietnam when it was established in 1955.

SEARCH AND DESTROY Operations in which troops searched an area to find and destroy Communist forces, hidden supplies, and living quarters.

SIEGE The act of surrounding and blockading the enemy to capture them.

STRATEGIC HAMLETS Fortified villages set up by US and ARVN forces to protect locals against attacks from Communist insurgents.

SURVEILLANCE Closely watching someone or something to obtain information about them.

TET The Buddhist Lunar New Year. Thousands of VC guerrillas attacked US and ARVN positions during the Tet holiday in 1968.

Tunnel rat gas mask

TUNNEL RATS The men who crawled into VC tunnels took this nickname.

VC Viet Cong, Communist guerrillas in South Vietnam.

VIETNAMESE POPULAR FORCES South Vietnamese military units made up of civilians.

VIETNAMIZATION US policy to turn over the fighting to the South Vietnamese Army; established by President Nixon.

ZIPPO A flamethrower that shot napalm; named for a type of cigarette lighter. A "Zippo job" was a mission to set Communist-held positions on fire.

Zippo in a firefight

Index

Acknowledgments

The publisher would like to thank the following for their help with making the book:
Clifford J. Rogers, Associate Professor of History, United States Military Academy; Steve R. Waddell, Associate Professor of History, United States Military Academy; Erika Rubel; Mark Tolf; David Mager; Michael Harris; Albert Moore; Doug Niven; Tim Page; Emma Naidoo; Jim Messinger; Bob Taylor; Justin Saffell; Ed Emering; Robert W. King; Ngo Vinh Long; Rev. Diedrik Nelson; Margie Ortiz and Terry Adams; Sema at Art-Hanoi; Ronnie Oldham; Jeff Lindsay; Tex Pantaleo; Robert H. Stoner, USNR (Ret.); Ron Toelke for cartography; Rob Stokes for relief mapping; Brian A. Benedict; Madeline Mancini and Madeline Farbman; Ian Fitzgerald for editorial assistance; Vagisha Pushp for picture research assistance; and Carron Brown for proofreading, indexing, and anglicization.

The publisher would like to thank the following for their kind permission to reproduce their images:
(Key: a-above; b-below/bottom; c-center; f-far; l-left; r-right; t-top)
Alamy Stock Photo: Avpics 34cl, LOU Collection 37tl, Military Collection 26–27tc, Associated Press/Hau Dinh 49crb, dpa picture alliance/Howard C. Breedlove—U.S. Army 34–35c, Associated Press/Horst Faas 10bl, GRANGER—Historical Picture Archive 50tr, CPA Media Pte Ltd/Pictures From History 70tc, INTERFOTO/History 10tr, Archive Image 25tr, RBM Vintage Images 24b, MediaPunch Inc 58cb, Photo12/Ann Ronan Picture Library 49tr, Associated Press/Claude Paris 69tl, Associated Press 10–11bc, 38–39bc, Photo12/Archives Snark 8tl, Associated Press/Sovfoto 22c, KEYSTONE Pictures USA 8–9bl, Associated Press/Sal Veder 58–59bc. **American Museum of Military History:** 33bl. **anothervietnam.com:** © Le Minh Truong, 22–23, 23cr, 25b, 40–41; © Vo Ann Khanh, 33br; © VNA, 44bl, 56–57tcl; © Duong Thanh Phong, 46tl, 60–61. **Art-hanoi.com:** 4crt, 19bc. **Australian War Memorial:** 69tcl. **Bernie Boston:** 50bl. **Boston University Archives:** 39tr. **Bridgeman Images:** Sovfoto/UIG 54ca; **brownwater-navy.com:** 42cr. **James Burmester:** 4clt, 15bc, 37br, 53cr. **Michael Burr:** 19r, 19bc. **Canadian Forces National Defense Ministry:** 4crb, 63cl. **CORBIS:** 35cr, 58bl; © Alinari Archives/CORBIS: 7tr; Bettman/CORBIS: 7cr, 8–9b, 9cl, 9cr, 16bc, 17cr,

20bc, 21br, 25tl, 31tr, 34bl, 38tl, 38bc, 39crt, 40cr, 43tr, 43cr, 45br, 50c, 51tr, 51cr, 51br, 53bl, 55tr, 57bl, 60bl, 63tr; © George Hall/CORBIS: 34br; © Jeremy Horner/CORBIS: 62tl; © Hulton-Deutsch Collection/CORBIS: 21t; © John R. Jones, Papilio/CORBIS: 46cr, 69bcl; © Catherine Karnow/CORBIS: 64bl; © Wally McNamee/CORBIS: 63cr; © Francoise de Mulder/CORBIS: 61tr; © Tim Page/CORBIS: 38cl, 62–63b; © Steve Raymer/CORBIS: 63b; Reuters/CORBIS: 69bl; © Roman Soumar/CORBIS: 46br; CORBIS SYGMA: 6tr; © Darren Whiteside/Reuters/CORBIS: 62bl. **DK Picture Library:** © DK Picture Library, courtesy Museum of American Political Life/University of Hartford: 51br (inset); © DK Picture Library, courtesy of Andrew L. Chernack: 23cl, 26 (scarf, canteen, pouch), 28cc (NVA knife); © David Mager/DK Picture Library, courtesy Mark Tolf: 2cr, 4tr, 4tc, 11cl, 15bl (inset), 27 lower cr, 27 upper c, 29t (M-1 carbine, access.), 29cl (cleaning kit and grenades), 29c (M-16 access.), 30br, 30tl (inset), 30bl, 31cr, 32cl, 32bc, 33cl, 35tr (patches), 37bc, 38ca, 41c (inset), 47 (all equipment), 51cr (inset), 55bl, 56ca (medal), 58bl, 65bl, 71r; © Stephen Oliver/DK Picture Library: 11bc; © Tim Ridley/DK Picture Library, courtesy of the Ministry of Defence Pattern Room, Nottingham: 2tcl, 28bcl (RPG-7 and accessories), 29tcr (M-16A1), 29bcr (M79); © Laura Wickenden/DK Picture Library: 46bcl. **Emering Coll.:** 2tr, 9c, 14c, 20tl, 37tc, 37te, 37tcr, 37cr, 37b, 59tc (POW & medal), 61cr, 62cr. **Folio, Inc. © Rob Crandall:** 68cl. **Michael Harris:** 62cl. **Getty Images:** Bettmann 6cl, 10cl, 13cr, 17tr, 18bl, 21br, 23tr, 32cr, 38bc, 39cla, 39cra, 42bl, 50–51bs, 51tl, 54–55cs, 57tr, 61tl, Corbis Historical/tim page 15br, 30cl, 30–31cs, 44–45bc, Rolls Press/Popperfoto 57ca, Keystone/Hulton Archive 57cla, Hindustan Times 50cl. **Lyndon Baines Johnson Pres. Lib.:** 15t, 48cl, 67cl. **John F. Kennedy Pres. Lib.:** 11tr. **Robert W. King:** 21tr (inset). **Coll. Ted Laurenson/©Diggitt McLaughlin:** 4tl, 16tl, 17br. **LJMilitaria:** 20c (inset), 56tl. **John P. Conway/vhpamuseum.org:** 32tl, 55cr, 71tl. **Library of Congress:** 10–11c, 11cr, 13tr, 14c, 14b, 16tr, 16bl, 16–17b, 18cl, 19b, 21cr, 21bl, 24b, 24cl, 26bl, 32cl, 39br, 45tc, 45cl, 45cr, 47tl, 47br, 49tr, 52c, 53cr, 53tc, 55br, 57tc, 57br, 59tr, 60cl (UPI), 61br, 66bc. © **Jeff Lindsay:** 65tl. **Mobile Riverine Forces Association/© Dan Dodd:** 42c (two patches, inset), 42cr, 43tl, 71b. **MPI Archives:** 2c, 50c; 59br, 65b. **Andrea Morland:**

68tr. **National Archives:** 2br, 6bl, 8tr, 9tr, 12cl, 14tl, 14cr, 15cr, 16cl, 16tr, 16bl, 16–17b, 18tr, 19cl, 23ca, 24tr, 25tr, 25cr, 26–27bc, 27tl, 27bl, 27ccr, 28tr, 28cl (grenades), 29br, 32br, 32bl, 33bc, 33tr, 35b, 36bl, 36–37, 39tcl, 40bl, 41tr, 41cr, 43tr, 44tr, 44cl, 45tr, 46tcl, 46bl, 52b, 55c, 60tr, 64–65 bkgnd, 65tr, 67b, 70br. **NPS/Terry Allen:** 68b, 68–69 bkgnd. **National Vietnam War Museum:** 34bl. **Naval Hist. Soc.:** 12cr, 12–13c. **Rev. Diedrik Nelson:** 4clb, 9bc, 56cl. **Ngo Vinh Long:** 7cl, 23br. **Shutterstock.com:** Everett Collection 20cl, 20–21c. **Stars and Stripes:** 39tl. **Texas Tech:** 25cl (inset), 29bl, 64tc, 64tr, 67tl, 70l; Anonymous Coll.: 58–59tc, 63tl, 64br; Peter Braestrup Coll.: 49br; Donald Jellema Coll.: 2tl, 28clt, 28bcr, 31b, 56br, 64br; Douglas Pike Coll.: 13tl, 15cl, 39cr (Cronkite), 48bl, 48cr, 54bc, 56bl; Brig. Gen. Edwin H. Simmons Coll.: 48–49bc. **Tim Page:** 1, 3, 15br, 30–31, 31cl, 62t. **Theodore Schweitzer III:** 58cl. **Tribune Media Service:** 38cr. **U.S. Air Force:** 21tcr, 34ca, 36tr. **U.S. Army:** 17ca, 27crb, 49tl, 53tl, 55tl, 56–57cc. **U.S. Army Ctr for Mil. Hist.:** 6–7tc, 11tl, 52c (inset), 65tl. **U.S. Army Mil. Hist. Inst.:** 65cr. **U.S. Navy:** 13cl, 42tr, 43cl, 58bc (nurse). **U.S. Navy, Naval Hist. Ctr:** 2 clb, 12c (inset), 12–13b, 66tr. **Vietnam Veterans Assoc. of Australia:** 63c. **VietnamWall.org:** 2bl, 2bc, 9tl (inset), 25tl (patch), 26ct, 27br, 28bl, 30clb, 33cr, 58tc (bracelet), 64tl, 65tl (bracelet & flute), 71cl. **Wikipedia:** Bibliography of Vietnamese official publications (1972) published by the Ministry of Culture, Education and Youth for the Republic of Vietnam 17tl. **www.aceworksbusy.com:** 4bl.

Cover images: Front: Alamy Stock Photo: dpa picture alliance b, GRANGER—Historical Picture Archive fcr, tc, UPI clb. **Bridgeman Images:** Peter Newark Military Pictures crb. **Dorling Kindersley:** Gary Ombler/Tim Parker tr, cr, Gary Ombler/Vietnam Rolling Thunder cra, br, Tim Ridley/Andrew L. Chernack fcla, fcl. **Dreamstime.com:** Tudor Antonel Adrian ca. **Getty Images:** Stuart Lutz/Gado ftr. **Getty Images/iStock:** lauradyoung cla, zim286 tl. **Shutterstock.com:** Andy Dean Photography c. **Back: Dorling Kindersley:** Gary Ombler/ Vietnam Rolling Thunder br. **Dreamstime.com:** Yuriy Merzlyakov cr. **Shutterstock.com:** Pete Hoffman cl. **Spine: Alamy Stock Photo:** dpa picture alliance.